LONG TIME DEAD

My Investigation into
the Unsolved Murder of
Ralph Wilson Snair

SUSAN MCIVER

FriesenPress

One Printers Way
Altona, MB R0G 0B0
Canada

www.friesenpress.com

Copyright © 2022 by Susan McIver, PhD
First Edition — 2022

All rights reserved.

No part of this publication may be reproduced in any form, or by any means, electronic or mechanical, including photocopying, recording, or any information browsing, storage, or retrieval system, without permission in writing from FriesenPress.

Cover photograph of cemetery in Sterling, Kansas, where Ralph Snair is buried.

ISBN
978-1-03-915113-0 (Hardcover)
978-1-03-915112-3 (Paperback)
978-1-03-915114-7 (eBook)

1. HISTORY, UNITED STATES, 20TH CENTURY

Distributed to the trade by The Ingram Book Company

In memory of Uncle Ralph and the people who loved him

Table of Contents

Acknowledgements vii
Introduction xi
PART I The Scene and Investigation 1
   Setting the Scene 2
   The Scene 9
   Wichita 24
   Unaccounted Time 33
   The Trip to Enid 41
   The Gun 46
PART II Autopsy 55
   Answers and Questions 56
   A Correction and Its Implication 61
   Suicide Revisited 65
PART III Ralph 79
   Not Just a Victim 80
   A Pioneer Family 82
   Youth and Early Adulthood 87
   Changes 91
   France 99
   Gassed 104

    Coming Home and Seeking Help............................109
    Dark Days..118
PART IV Suspects 125
    Warren Arthur Girvin 126
    Ralph Howell Campbell 132
    John Lawrence Faith...143
    The Mysterious Mr. Weasner 146
PART V Final Thoughts.............................. 151
    Two Small Scars..152
    Unresolved 160
    Family Grief..166
Appendices
    Appendix 1 Psychological Impact
    of Military Conflict 170
    Appendix 2 Cross-Dressing 174
    Appendix 3 Drugs in Kansas 177
    Appendix 4 The Tale of Two Brothers
    and the Taste of Corn Flakes....................................181
References 189
About the Author....................................... 193

Acknowledgements

I am most grateful that my great aunt Edna Wilson meticulously collected family postcards and that my cousin Don McCrory compiled them into an album. The idea for this book originated with the album and a reunion of cousins organized by Don and his brother Phil McCrory. I am also grateful to Vicki Kay, daughter of Fravel Snair *and* Ralph's niece, for her encouragement and willingness to share family history. Thanks to my sister, Dorothy Harp, for her support and to Rev. Robert McFarland and Roberta McFarland for adding to my knowledge of the Snair family in Zenda and Sterling.

Laura Graham, general counsel, and Sheila Sawyer-Tyler, legal assistant, of the Kansas Bureau of Investigation, each provided invaluable assistance in locating and making Ralph's file available. Karen Robb of the Harvey County coroner's office found both Ralph's autopsy report and the coroner's report in a dusty corner of the storage room a year after my initial inquiry. Thank you, Laura, Sheila, and Karen—your contributions were special highlights along the way. Thanks also to Kim Moon for checking the records of the Harvey County Sheriff Office.

My long-held opinion that Kansans are some of the nicest people in the world was confirmed by Donna Werner, Betty Devoe, Bonnie Bailey, and the ladies in the telephone office, all residents of Zenda, and Amy Gard and Pam Smith of Sterling.

A special word of thanks to Harvey County historian Darren J. McMannis, who so willingly shared historical newspaper accounts, and also to Nancy Wilkison, Dede Brossard, and Norma Cowie, who provided background information.

Special mention goes to Harry Goldhar for our many discussions and his editorial input. Thanks also to Dr. Khati Hendry for reviewing the autopsy report, to Jeff Everden, funeral director, for information on the embalming process, and to Christian Nuessler and Roch Fortin for their most helpful insights gained from their experience as law enforcement officers.

And finally, I want to thank my partner, Robin Wyndham. Her willingness to spend endless hours hashing over every possible angle and detail of Ralph's life and murder, her unflagging encouragement, and her skill as an editor made this book possible.

Acknowledgements

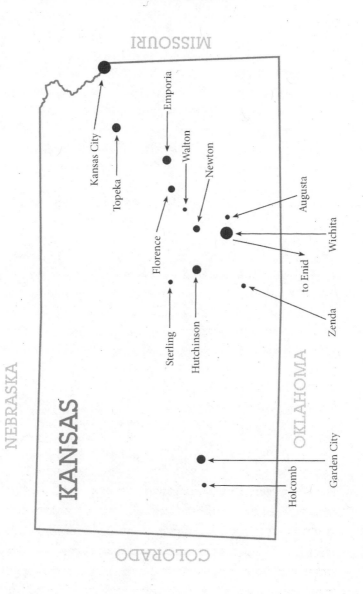

Map of Kansas with relevant locations indicated.

Long Time Dead

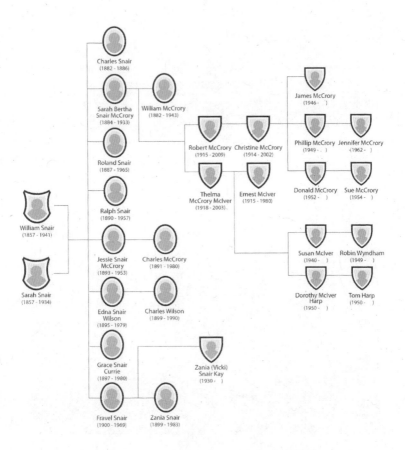

Descendants of William and Sarah Snair mentioned in text.

Introduction

I knew about murder from the time I was a young child. The husband of my deceased aunt killed his second wife. My aunt had died in a head-on car crash seven years before, leaving five children. Her husband remarried, and it was this woman whom he beat to death with a hammer. There was no question of his guilt. He was arrested, convicted, and sentenced. Many years later, he was paroled and lived the few remaining years of his life in a trailer house on the farm of his eldest daughter.

Soon after the murder, his three youngest daughters, my first cousins, came to live with my family. The oldest girl married at 15, with the permission of my father, her legal guardian. The younger two girls remained with us until it became financially impossible for my parents to support them, and they were placed in a foster home. Regardless of their father's crime, the girls grew into women who led useful, law-abiding lives.

The impact on my parents and on the grandmother and aunt I had in common with my cousins was considerable. The murder even influenced the way our aunt, who died 50 years after the murder, made her will, leaving out my cousins because of their father's crime. As would be expected, the impact has faded until now I wonder if my nieces and nephews, let alone their children, even know that this murder occurred in our family.

The murder of my great uncle, Ralph Wilson Snair, was entirely different. He was the victim, not the perpetrator. He was older and had no children. There was no apparent reason, such as domestic strife, for the crime. The murderer has never been identified nor arrested and brought to justice. The people most directly affected were his brothers and sisters, and my mother and her brother.

Saturday morning of Easter Weekend in 1957, the phone rang in my childhood home in San Bernardino, California. It was my mother's brother, Bob, in Kansas. Uncle Ralph had been shot to death. His body had been found in a rented car at the side of a road, miles from where he lived. Nothing similar had ever happened in my mother's family. Stunned by the news, my mother heard Bob say the police were to meet with him and Ralph's sisters, Edna and Grace, later that day.

During phone calls to Edna and Grace, my parents never once hesitated to say we would be making the trip to Kansas. After all, Ralph, a life-long bachelor, who doted on his nieces and nephews, was my mother's favourite uncle and a loved member of a close-knit family. A building contractor, Dad planned the work schedule for his crew while we would be away. Mother, a homemaker, made sure the house was in order and we had clean clothes and appropriate outfits for

Introduction

Ralph's funeral. My seven-year-old sister, Dorothy, and I, a junior in high school, would miss school.

On the Monday after Easter, we packed our Chevy Impala and headed east across the Mojave Desert. We drove across the desert at night to avoid the heat of the day. Cars at that time did not have air conditioning. Twelve years earlier, with the ink barely dry on the document signed by the Japanese ending the Second World War, my parents and I had made the same trip travelling west. In the intervening years, we had made annual trips to Kansas as my parents adjusted to life in California while maintaining close contact with the relatives they had left behind.

Tears ran down Edna and Grace's cheeks as they embraced us when we arrived. There were hugs and tears for everyone as other family members—Ralph's younger brother from New Jersey, his older brother from Colorado, and nieces, nephews, and cousins from around Kansas—came to honour and remember Ralph. Shock and sadness permeated the air. Questions and speculations dominated the conversations. Imprinted in my memory was Uncle Bob reporting that the police had said to him, "We know who did it; we just can't prove it."

On Thursday, April 25, 1957, friends and community members gathered with the family at the white wood-frame Reformed Presbyterian Church in Sterling for the funeral. This was the same church where, for years, Ralph had attended Sunday services and gone to weddings and funerals. My mother had been raised in that church, and as a small child, I had been the flower girl at my Uncle Bob's wedding.

Long Time Dead

The years passed, and it became apparent that Ralph's murder would most likely never be solved. Gradually grief and speculation diminished, but the question of "who did it?" persisted. Over the years, Edna, Grace, my parents, and Bob all died. Dorothy grew up, went to university, married, and became a mother and grandmother. I graduated from university, earned a doctorate, and moved to Canada, where I was a professor and research scientist and later a coroner and writer.

It was not until the summer of 2017 that my interest in Ralph's murder was renewed. The occasion was a gathering of first cousins in Hutchinson, Kansas. The first afternoon my partner, Robin Wyndham, and I from British Columbia, and Don McCrory and his wife, Sue, from Michigan met at the home of Phil and Jenn McCrory in Hutchinson. That evening we were joined by my sister, Dorothy Harp, and her husband, Tom, from California and Phil and Don's older brother, Jim, who lived in Sterling, Kansas.

During the afternoon, Don showed us an album he had organized containing over 300 postcards our great aunt Edna had saved. The album contains postcards that bear postmarks from 1903 through the 1970s and include cards to and from Ralph over four decades. As I examined the dog-eared, yellowed postcards in Phil and Jenn's living room that warm July afternoon, I realized how little I knew about the gentle man I remembered. There were many incidents Ralph mentioned in the postcards I had known nothing about.

Don also shared two photocopied newspaper clippings about Ralph's death, including an article by Bill Hazlett that

Introduction

appeared in the *Wichita Beacon* on April 21, 1957. Hazlett quoted Harvey County Sheriff Weldon Morford as saying that the bullet entered Snair's head from above and behind the right ear "in such a way that it would have been almost impossible for him to have shot himself, unless he turned the pistol upside down."

Sue made a "pistol" with her fingers, trying to re-enact how the bullet could have entered Ralph's head where the sheriff said it did. "Someone should write a book," she said, as we munched chips and discussed the murder. Her statement combined with the postcard album and the news clippings made me start to think about the possibility. Over the years, I have had a lot of people tell me I should write various articles and books, but this was the first time I did not dismiss the idea out of hand.

On the four-day drive back to our home in British Columbia, Robin and I discussed at length the reunion and the possibility of a book. As wheat fields turned to mountains and then to the semi-arid landscape of the South Okanagan, we wondered what information might still exist so many years after Ralph's death. How could we find out? What type of book might it become? And most importantly did I want to do it? We both knew from writing two previous books how much work and dedication are required. By the time we pulled into our driveway, I knew I was going to try to pull together what information existed and see if it might result in a book.

In the spring of 2018, Robin and I drove to Kansas again so that I could retrace Ralph's footsteps as much as possible. His birthplace at the family homestead, the town where he spent his childhood, and the places where he lived and worked in later life were all visited and explored. I located the place where his body was found—along a two-lane asphalt road with fields on one side and more fields and railroad tracks on the other. I visited his grave in the Sterling Cemetery, where many of my extended family are buried. In November 2018, I flew to Topeka to examine Ralph's file at the headquarters of the Kansas Bureau of Investigation.

Hundreds of hours were spent compiling information, reading old newspaper accounts, and looking up information on the computer. I read stacks of books about people who intentionally kill other people—serial killers, spur-of-the-moment killers, people who kill for no apparent reason, and hired killers. I explored the field of forensic psychology and read about the 1918 Influenza pandemic and the First World War, the development of American medicine, and social trends, such as eugenics and illicit drug use.

Robin and I spent endless hours talking about every piece, even the tiniest bit, of information I found. What had shaped the man Ralph became? What role did his military service and injury during the First World War play in his life and perhaps death? What influence did the social attitudes and medical concepts of the day have? And most of all how did such a simple-living Christian man, a retired church custodian, come to die of a gunshot to the head at the side of a highway in rural Kansas?

This is the story of a murder that has remained unsolved for over 60 years.

PART I

The Scene and Investigation

Setting the Scene

A few weeks after returning home from the reunion with my cousins, I began looking for answers to the fundamental question Robin and I had asked ourselves on the long drive from Kansas. What information might still exist so many years after Ralph's death? My initial attempts to answer this question were discouraging.

My first query was to the coroner's office in Harvey County, Kansas, the county in which Ralph's body had been found. Did they have a report? As a former coroner in British Columbia, I had written many reports and knew they contain valuable information. In October 2017, I received a response from Karen Robb, a county death investigator. I was pleased to receive her email but disappointed with the contents. Ms. Robb wrote that her records in the database only went back to 1959, two years after Ralph's death. "That doesn't mean we don't have anything, although that's possible," she wrote. She told me that the Coroner's Office shared storage space with the County Sheriff's Office, and she would check as to the whereabouts of Ralph's records.

Setting the Scene

Ms. Robb also suggested other possible sources of information, such as the county district court and the name of a local historian, Darren McMannis. In November 2017, Dawn Varga of the district court notified me that as far as she could tell coroners' reports went back only to 1965. "I will ask the chief clerk if she knows where there may be other reports," she wrote. Due to technical problems, I did not hear from Mr. McMannis for several months. When I did, however, he gave me valuable information leading to newspaper articles that related to Ralph's death. A flicker of light.

In fall 2017, I contacted the Harvey County Sheriff's Office. In response, records clerk Kim Moon wrote, "I don't have reports from before 1959. From what I have been told there was no record keeping before then. The 1959 thru 60's reports are hit and miss. Several very short reports, not much info." Was the sheriff's report, if it existed, buried in the dust bin of time? Ms. Moon and I exchanged emails for a couple of years. In summer 2019, Ms. Moon wrote that Sheriff Gay and she would have another look after the remodelling of their office had been done. I have not heard from her since.

The first promising lead came when I contacted the Legal Division of the Kansas Bureau of Investigation in Topeka. Ms. Laura Graham, general counsel AAG of the KBI, gave me the welcome news that the agency did have a file on Ralph Snair. Due to the age of the case, however, it was on microfiche and needed to be digitized. Once I paid the fee in early 2018 and the file was digitized, Ms. Graham sent me a few extracts. She could not release the entire file because the case was still open.

And then the proverbial tide turned. On September 10, 2018, almost a year after my initial contact, I received an email from Karen Robb. "Last Friday Deena, our District Court Clerk, brought me some old Autopsy Reports and I was thrilled to see the Coroner's Report of Investigation and a set of autopsy photograph! Please let me know if you would like them." These reports anchored my investigation into Ralph's case. They validated crucial information Ms. Graham had told me and gave me additional evidence about the murder itself and insights into Ralph as a person, not just as a loved uncle or a murder victim.

In November 2018, Ms. Graham emailed that, because I was a relative and undertaking a serious project, I could view the KBI file in person if I were to come to Topeka. I was elated. The email arrived on my birthday—a most appreciated gift. Later that month, I flew to Topeka on the heels of a blizzard. The temperature outside was more than compensated for by Ms. Graham and her legal assistant Sheila Sawyer-Tyler's warm welcome and helpfulness.

The danger associated with the KBI's work was first apparent from the strict security measures needed to enter the building. The several locked doors between the spare office I was using and the ladies' room necessitated that Ms. Sawyer-Tyler, who had the keys, had to escort me to the washroom. The main hallway contains display cases with memorabilia of famous crimes involving the KBI. The dust cover of Truman Capote's book *In Cold Blood*,[1] a detailed account of the 1959 murders of the Cutler family, is in a

Setting the Scene

display case. It was particularly chilling to see the knife with which Perry Smith cut Herb Cutler's throat and the shotgun used to shoot Cutler and the other three members of his family on their farm near Holcomb, Kansas.

Although I was not permitted to photograph or photocopy the file, I could copy it by hand and spent the better part of three days writing down every word. I was somewhat surprised by the brevity of the file, and Ms. Graham considered it to be one of the shortest she had seen. In subsequent close examination, I came to suspect that parts of the file could be missing; for example, references are made to follow-up investigations, yet there are no reports of those investigations in the file I received. The reason(s) for these suspected missing parts is not apparent. They could have been lost over time or perhaps they were never included.

Only in late 2019 did I come to understand that the missing sheriff's file and perhaps the short KBI file might be indictive of systemic poor record keeping. In his book *And Every Word is True,* with deceased KBI Agent Harold Nye's son, Ronald R. Nye, Gary McAvoy wrote on p. 57:[2]

> Indeed, Logan Sanford, director of the KBI until 1969, once lamented, "Law-enforcement and crime records in Kansas through the years have been seriously inadequate. . . . In many cases an outgoing police chief or sheriff just destroyed his records or took them with him. We've found many cases in the state where a

crime has been committed but where there
is not a written record."

Not only was the sheriff's written account of the investigation missing, but also information sent to him as noted in the KBI file. In addition, physical items associated with the case, such as the gun and Ralph's hat and billfold, could not be found. The missing files and physical evidence are particularly egregious considering this case is unsolved and remains open. Evidence is normally retained until the perpetrators are tried in a court of law.

An increasing number of cold cases are now being solved because even old and miniscule amounts of DNA associated with the victim or crime scene can identify the killer. Genetic genealogy is being used to narrow the search for perpetrators through identification of their relatives using DNA banks of the general population. The unfortunate loss of physical evidence in Ralph's case eliminates the possibility of ever using DNA analysis to positively identify his killer. This is one of the most disappointing aspects of my investigation. Would I be writing this book if DNA analysis and other modern forensic techniques, such as the detection of microscopic pieces of evidence, telephone tracing, and psychological profiling, had been available?

Investigators of the day did have basic forensic tools at their disposal, such as techniques for detecting fingerprints and gunshot residue. The coroner and the pathologist who conducted the autopsy provided medical information. Investigators relied heavily on the proverbial "shoe leather." These techniques are reminiscent of the gritty realism of the

Setting the Scene

television show *Dragnet,* popular in the 1950s and 1960s, featuring Sergeant Joe Friday of the Los Angeles Police Department. During my investigation, I had to reset my expectations from those associated with the high-tech procedures yielding definitive and instantly available results portrayed in the *Crime Scene Investigation (CSI)* television series of the 21st century to those of the 1950s.

The paucity of information in Ralph's case makes the scrutiny of the information that does exist especially important. This starts with a detailed account of the scene in the next chapter. Careful examination of a crime scene in search of evidence about the perpetrator is a fundamental concept of criminal investigations. In the latter part of the 20th century, social science disciplines, such as psychology, criminology, and sociology, began to be used extensively in conjunction with traditional criminal investigation methods to better understand criminal behaviour and the factors that influence it.

A widely recognized outcome of this trend was the establishment of the FBI's Behavioral Analysis Unit at Quantico, Virginia. The unit and its founder, the legendary profiler John Douglas, served as a basis for the popular American crime drama series *Criminal Minds*, which ran on television from 2005 to 2020.

In summarizing the work of crime scene profilers, Katherine Ramsland wrote on p. 36 in her book[3] *The Forensic Psychology of Criminal Minds:*

> They (profilers) consider whether a weapon
> was brought to the scene or taken away, the

state of the scene(s), the type of wounds inflicted on the victim, risks the offender took, his or her method of controlling the victim, and evidence that the incident may be staged to look like something else. In addition, there may be indications that the offender has one or more partners.

The first generally recognized application of criminal profile techniques dates from 1888 when London physicians George Phillips and Thomas Bond used autopsy results and crime scene evidence to make informed predictions about the personality, behavioural characteristics, and lifestyle of the legendary serial killer Jack the Ripper. Based on available forensic evidence, Dr. Bond stated that Jack the Ripper had no medical training or knowledge of anatomy, despite the killer's extensive cutting and mutilation of his victims. Law enforcement authorities had previously thought the murderer was either a physician or had medical training because he had removed internal organs and slashed the women. It will never be known if Dr. Bond's conclusions were correct. Like the murder of Ralph Snair, the Ripper murders remain unsolved.

The Scene

US Highway 50 stretches across the country for 3000 miles from California to Maryland. It was created in 1926 as part of the original United States Highway system. In Kansas, Highway 50 generally follows the route of the old Santa Fe Trail from the Colorado State line to Dodge City where the trail veers northeast, while the highway continues straight east to Newton in the centre of the state. Newton, an agriculture-based town, had about 13,000 inhabitants n 1957 and is the seat of Harvey County.

Seven miles northeast of Newton is the tiny town of Walton, which 220 people called home in the 1950s. The town and US 50 haven't changed much since then. Walton has grown by about 100 inhabitants, and its most prominent feature continues to be grain elevators visible from the site where Ralph's body was found, two miles east of the town near the intersection of Highway 50 and an unpaved country road. Highway 50 is still a two-lane asphalt highway that cuts through wheat fields with the Burlington Northern Santa Fe Railway tracks on the south side. The only siding in the area off the single-track railway enters Walton from the west and dead ends at the

Long Time Dead

grain elevators. The highway continues northeast from Walton through the small towns of Peabody and Florence to the City of Emporia and eventually reaches Kansas City as Interstate 35.

Before first light on Good Friday, April 19, 1957, Kenneth Armstrong headed out on the first of two deliveries for the Sunbeam Bread Company of Newton. His route took him east along Highway 50 toward Emporia. At 4:30 a.m., Armstrong noticed a car parked on the north side of Highway 50 about two miles east of Walton. He later told the sheriff he had seen the car three more times that morning.

Shoulder of Highway 50 near site where the rented car containing Ralph's body was found.

In the afternoon, two boys were hunting in a field near the car and shot a rabbit. "If there is anybody asleep in that car, that ought to waken him," one of the boys said, as the

The Scene

gun went off. The boys neither fired in the direction of the car nor saw anyone in or around it.

Shortly after 7:00 p.m., Trooper Bernard Powell of the Kansas Highway Patrol was on a routine patrol when he noticed a 1956 blue Ford sedan parked on the shoulder of Highway 50. The car was found slightly west of the intersection of the highway and a country road, and parked so its left side was about nine feet from the pavement slab. It faced west toward Walton. The exterior of the car did not show any signs of damage, and there was no sign of disturbance in the area around it. Powell pulled up behind the car, noted the 1957 Kansas licence plate number SG-7011, and stepped out of his car. His routine patrol was about to become a murder investigation.

Shining a flashlight into the car window, Trooper Powell saw the body of a man in the front seat. The body was visible only when looking into the car at close range and was reclined to the left so that the head rested on the arm rest on the driver's door. The legs were spread so that the right foot was near the right-side panel beneath the dash and the left foot near the left panel. The man had been shot in the head, apparently, while sitting upright. (The Kansas Highway Patrol was unable to locate any report of this incident in its investigative reports.)

Trooper Powell notified authorities at the Highway Patrol Office in Wichita, who, in turn, contacted Harvey County officials in Newton. Sheriff Weldon Morford, Undersheriff Walter Hillman, and Coroner M. C. Martin, M.D. soon arrived at the scene. Trooper Powell and Coroner Martin photographed the exterior of the car and its interior with the body in place.

Long Time Dead

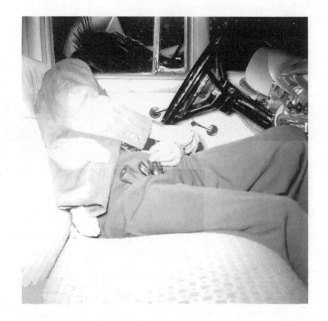

Body in the car. Courtesy of Harvey Co. Coroner's Office.

The Scene

Body in the car. Photo taken with driver's side door open.
Courtesy of Harvey Co. Coroner's Office.

Coroner Martin's report is the only existing firsthand account written by anyone at the scene. Information reported in newspapers was based primarily on conversations with Sheriff Morford, and as previously mentioned, any reports he might have written no longer exist. Description of the scene on the evening of April 19 in the KBI file is based on second-hand information.

Realizing the case was a possible homicide, Coroner Martin and Sheriff Morford agreed to call the KBI in Topeka for assistance. Agent James Kline, the lead KBI investigator, drove to Newton, arriving shortly after midnight. He would have passed the scene in the dark after the body and car had been removed. KBI Agent Paul Lansdowne joined the investigation at 6:00 a.m. the next morning in Wichita.

Upon notifying the motor vehicle registration department, investigators learned that the licence plate had been issued to the car rental agency, U-Drive-It Service, on North Broadway in Wichita. When investigators called the agency, two young men from there went immediately to the scene. They showed the coroner the Certificate of Title and told him the licence plate number before they had a chance to see it themselves. The young men said the car had been rented to a Ralph Wilson Snair of North Chautauqua Avenue, Wichita, two days before on April 17 and he had driven away at 2:59 p.m.

Regarding the body, Coroner Martin wrote:

> The man had been shot in the head but a relatively small amount of blood was visible. He laid with his head against the left door of the car, with his head lying upon the armrest as a pillow.
>
> When shot, he had not been under the wheel in a driving position, but had been sitting, actually, to the right of the middle of the front seat. It is not known whether he was sitting in that position or was placed in that fashion to allow space for his head to rest against the left door.

The Scene

The last sentence implies that Ralph may have been in the driver's seat and pulled to the centre after being shot. This may have been done to allow his body to fall to the left below the line of sight. The lack of an exit wound would explain why the left side window was not shattered or splattered with blood.

As reported by the *Evening Kansan-Republican* on Monday, April 22, all four of the car's doors were closed; the back doors were locked, and the front doors unlocked. All windows in the car were up. The ignition was turned off. The same article reported that the car key was attached to the murdered man's belt. This statement is almost certainly incorrect. Coroner Martin reported that a key chain and a Yale key to the man's room in Wichita were the only items other than clothing found on the body. The coroner's comments of a room key, not a car key, being found are substantiated by the fact that in the United States, the Yale company did not manufacture keys for automobiles.

The whereabouts of the car key remains a mystery. In photographs, Ralph's knee is seen to cover the portion of the dash where the car key would have been inserted, so it is impossible to tell if the key was in the ignition. If it was not in the ignition or found on Ralph's person, then it was likely taken by someone involved in the murder, who discarded it.

A .22 calibre Iver Johnson target pistol with a 6-inch barrel was lying in Ralph's lap beneath his crossed hands. The barrel of the gun pointed toward the car's left front window. In photographs, the gun appears to be almost upside down. Ralph's left hand was lying on the top of the gun while his right hand was lying on the left. The location of the gun caused investigators to consider the possibility that Ralph had shot himself. Coroner Martin concluded that Ralph had been murdered and had not committed suicide. In his words:

> At first glance, this was a picture of a suicide but as the true view came before us, it added up to a very crude attempt to simulate a suicide.

Staging the scene to appear as a suicide is commonly done by killers to avoid the detailed, thorough investigation associated with a homicide.

When he was shot, Ralph was wearing a blue herringbone suit coat, a light brown shirt, short-sleeved long underwear, brown trousers, and oxfords. Both shoes had metatarsal arch supports in them. He had on gold metal-framed glasses and a brown felt hat.

Agent Kline reported details about the hat:

> Found that the brown felt hat had two bullet holes in the right side--both made by the same bullet. There was a hole in the right side of the brim near the edge & from there had entered the crown of the hat. The hat had apparently been turned up when the bullet had been fired. A large amount of powder residue appeared around the holes which indicated that the gun had been held at close range.

The Scene

Over a year after the murder on June 14, 1958, Ralph's older brother, Roland Snair, a teacher in Greeley, Colorado, wrote to Agent Kline:

> At the time of the tragedy we were told by the Harvey Co. authorities that when they found Ralph his hat had been placed on his head backwards, that the bullet hole in the hat did not lineup with the hole in his head.

Agent Kline replied that the hat could have been placed in the reverse position by unknown persons or come to rest in that position with the movement of the body. By "movement of the body" did he mean the reclining of Ralph's body from an upright position to coming to rest on the driver's side door when he was shot? It is difficult to visualize how this slumping could have caused the hat to turn 180 degrees and remain on Ralph's head. Or was Agent Kline suggesting the body had been moved, perhaps in sliding it from the driver's position to the middle of the front seat, and the hat repositioned by an unknown person? Another possibility is that in his initial examination of the car, Trooper Powell opened the driver's side door, allowing Ralph's hat to fall off his head. He then replaced the hat in the 180-degree reverse position in which it was reported to have been found.

Only two items were reported being found in the car other than the gun and those on Ralph's body. Sheriff Morford found two receipts for purchase of gasoline in the car's glove compartment. The first purchase was made on

Long Time Dead

the morning of February 18 at the Mecca Service Station, 7th Street and Dearborn Avenue in Augusta, Kansas, and the second purchase in the evening of the same day at the Kurtz "66" Service Station, Highway 50S and 77th Street in Florence, Kansas.

A front-page story on April 23, 1957, in the *Evening Kansan-Republican* reported:

> Nearby on the seat was a while linen handkerchief, probably removed from the slain man's pocket. It is believed the killer wiped tell tale fingerprints from the gun before leaving the scene. No identifying marks were found on the handkerchief.

Neither the KBI agents nor the coroner mentioned a white handkerchief in their reports.

Two days later, an article in the same newspaper reported:

> Although the murder weapon was wiped clear of fingerprints, officers found several prints in the car and these are now being run through the mill for possible identification purposes.

There was no further mention anywhere of tests to identify the fingerprints found in the car.

As is visible in photographs and mentioned in reports, all four pockets of Ralph's suit coat and trousers were turned inside out. It is not clear whether the inside out pockets

The Scene

indicated the killer tried to make the scene look like a robbery or, in fact, there had been a robbery or even if Ralph had turned them out himself.

Agent Kline wrote to Roland, in a letter dated June 25, 1958:

> This [pockets inside out] in itself might indicate robbery until you give it some thought. I have never seen nor heard of a robbery in which this was done. Ordinarily a thief will take what he wants from a victim's pockets without having to go to all of this trouble.

Support for the possibility of robbery came when investigators returned to the scene the day after discovery of the body and Agent Kline found a brown leather billfold in a roadside ditch. The billfold contained identification papers for Ralph Wilson Snair and a receipt for the deposit he had made on the rental car. No money was found, even though Ralph was reported by Mr. David Stavniak, one of the young men at the car rental agency, to have had considerable cash when he rented the car on the preceding Tuesday afternoon. The day after the discovery of Ralph's body, Mr. Stavniak modified his story saying the apparent "considerable cash" could have been a large number of small denomination bills. Regardless of the bills' denomination, the money had apparently been taken. In addition, Mr. Stavniak's observation of Ralph having numerous bills was out of character for a man known to be frugal and to never carry large amounts of money.

Even if a robbery did occur, it is unknown whether it was the motive for the murder or that the killer decided to take the money as a bonus for his work.

The billfold was found about 140 feet west of where the car had been parked and about 20 feet north of the slab. To put the distance in perspective, 140 feet is 46.6 yards, almost half the length of a football field. This strongly suggests the billfold had been discarded by someone leaving the scene going toward Walton. It could have been tossed from the right-side window by a passenger in a get-away car. There is no record of the billfold having been checked for fingerprints.

On the evening of April 19, the ambulance from the Draper Funeral Home driven by Orville Zellers arrived at about 8:25 p.m. Zellers was accompanied by the owner of the funeral home, Irwin Draper. The body was removed to the funeral home in Newton for examination. The car was picked up by Nordstrom-Smuck Ford Agency from Newton and stored until it could be processed by the police. It was eventually released to the rental agency.

In view of the initial findings, Coroner Martin placed the case in the hands of Harvey County Attorney John Plummer, Sheriff Morford, and the Kansas Bureau of Investigation. Arrangements were made for an autopsy to be done by Dr. W.P. Callahan or his assistant, Dr. Karl M. Neudorfer, both working in Wichita.

In his report dated April 21, 1957, Coroner Martin discussed the difficulty he faced in determining the time of death. When he examined the body at the scene, rigor mortis had been at its height. It was disappearing a couple

The Scene

of hours later, sometime between 9:00 and 9:30 p.m., at the funeral home in Newton. Coroner Martin wrote that allowing for a ten-hour maximum time for formation of rigor mortis and another ten-hour maximum for its disappearance, the man could have been killed as early as 1:30 a.m. on April 19.

After considering information from the scene, examining the body at the funeral home, and learning autopsy results, Coroner Martin concluded:

> It is the opinion of the Coroner that Mr. Ralph Snair, age 67, (S.S.# 512-22-0140) met his death from a gunshot wound of the head, inflicted feloniously by parties unknown at this time; that, as of this time, no reason for the criminal act is known other than robbery.

In assessing the evidence, retired Royal Canadian Mounted Police officer Christian Nuessler, pointed out that the scene had not been secured during the roughly 18 hours from the time Ralph was shot until Trooper Powell found his body. Someone other than the killer may have searched the body for valuables, turned the pockets inside out, and thrown the billfold in the ditch. If he had been robbed, Ralph could have possibly turned his pockets inside out himself to demonstrate there was nothing in them. Perhaps someone had wiped fingerprints from the gun with the handkerchief and placed it in Ralph's lap. And who, if anyone, put Ralph's hat on backwards after he had been shot. But then the killer may have done all those things.

Many people had access to the scene, from those passing by on foot to those in cars and trucks. Bread delivery man Kenneth Armstrong said he had seen the car four times on April 19, starting at 4:30 a.m. Several other motorists told the sheriff they had seen the car. The two boys hunting in the area in the afternoon said they did not see anyone around the car. They gave the sheriff the names of four men they had seen in the general area and said they had spoken with two of the men. The sheriff was to speak with the men, but nothing further was reported. Sheriff Morford did not learn of the incident involving the boys until May 3, two weeks after the discovery of Ralph's body, as reported by the *Evening Kansan-Republican* on May 4. No reason was given for this delay.

Neither the KBI file nor the coroner's report mentions how the killer(s) left the scene. If the departure was by car, there are two possible scenarios. One is a rendezvous with Ralph had been planned at the site where the body was found. The killer arrived in his own car, shot Ralph, and left in the same car. Another possibility is that the killer met Ralph elsewhere, travelled with him to the site where he shot, and was then picked up by an associate driving another car.

Was the killer someone on foot, such as a hitch hiker? Did Ralph pick up someone or perhaps stopped the car to relieve himself and encountered his murderer by chance? It is difficult to imagine how anyone could have hitch hiked or walked away without being noticed. This would have

The Scene

been especially true in a rural farming area, where people often rise before the sun, know the routines of neighbours, and take particular notice of strangers. Ralph's murder was widely known, so it seems reasonable to think that anyone who had picked up a hitch hiker or had seen anyone walking along the road would have contacted the police.

There is the possibility, although slim, that the proximity between Highway 50 and the single-track railway that runs parallel was a factor. Criminal activity associated with railroad lines is well known—that is, someone riding the rails leaves the train, commits a crime as a robbery or murder, and departs the scene on the next train, making apprehension almost impossible. The only siding that would facilitate getting on and off the train by anyone riding illegally is the short, dead-end siding in Walton, approximately two miles away.

Wichita

Information about Ralph's activities in the weeks preceding his death began to emerge as dawn approached the day after the discovery of his body. At 3:00 a.m., on April 20, Sheriff Morford, Agent Kline, and Harvey County Attorney John Plummer left for Wichita, the state's largest city, located 27 miles directly south of Newton. They were joined by KBI Agent Paul Lansdowne and Sedgwick County Attorney Warner Moore.

The investigators' first stop was the city's police department, where they left the revolver and the paraffin casts taken of Ralph's hands for examination by experts. A Wichita Police Department file of this forensic examination was not generated because the examination had been requested by Sheriff Morford and the KBI. Wichita detectives were not called into the case. Results were reported to the sheriff and recorded in the KBI file. The gun would have been returned to the Harvey County Sheriff's Office.

Upon checking the WPD's files, the only report the sheriff and KBI agents found concerning Ralph was of the accident on October 13, 1943, when he was struck by an automobile and hospitalized with a broken leg. At that time, he was living at the Stackman Apartments on North Main Street. According to the city directory, Ralph was currently residing on North Chautauqua Avenue, the same address Ralph had given to the owners of the car rental agency.

About 4:00 a.m., the officers, accompanied by Lieutenant William Overman of the Uniformed Division of the WPD, went to the Chautauqua address and spoke with owners, Garrett A. and Edna Mae Girvin. Their son, Warren A. Girvin, who lived in Raytown, Missouri, was also present. He would later become a suspect in the murder case. The officers described the dead man, and the Girvins confirmed that he was Ralph Snair.

Mrs. Girvin said they had rented an upstairs apartment to Ralph for the past two years and that he paid part of his rent by working in the yard and taking care of the house. She described Ralph as a 67-year-old man, who was quiet, reserved, and deeply religious, and abstained from alcohol and tobacco. He was frugal and never carried large amounts of money. From all indications, Ralph got along well with the family, was a good tenant, and performed his tasks in the yard and house well. Mrs. Girvin told investigators that Ralph was afraid of guns and expressed fear even at the sound of a gunshot.

According to Mrs. Girvin, Ralph had worked as an assistant custodian at the College Hill Methodist Church, located diagonally across the nearest corner to the Girvin residence. He had retired from his fulltime position in August 1956 and continued to work part time. Ralph had few friends, none of them close. She thought his closest associate would have been the church's head custodian, Mr. Way.

Long Time Dead

Mrs. Girvin told investigators of something that happened three days before Trooper Powell found the body. In retrospect, what she said was not only unusual but was also likely key to unravelling the events leading to Ralph's murder.

On Tuesday, February 16, Mrs. Girvin had gone to the hairdresser's at 10:30 a.m.; Ralph was home at the time. When she returned at 2:15 p.m., he was gone. She found a note from him which read:

> Mrs. Girvin—I got a call this morning from Mr. Weasner wanting me to come over to Newton and help him. If I don't get back here tomorrow I will be back Thursday sometime. Ralph

The note was the last contact of any type the Girvins had with Ralph. It was given to Agent Kline.

Mr. Girvin told officers that when Ralph had neither returned home nor called by Friday evening, his wife had told him that she had a feeling something had happened to him. Her premonition was eerily correct because that was the evening Trooper Powell discovered Ralph's body.

In the middle of March, about a month before his murder, Ralph mentioned to Mrs. Girvin he had met an old friend he had known when he lived on North Main Street. Near the end of March, he told her that a friend of his wanted him to drive to Enid, Oklahoma. In particular, the friend asked Ralph to rent a car and haul something back for him. Subsequently, Ralph did rent a car and drive

Wichita

to Enid. The Girvins suggested the man from North Main Street, the person who accompanied Ralph to Enid, and the man named Weasner mentioned in the note were the same person.

Ralph's sisters, Edna Wilson of Hutchinson and Grace Currie of Sterling, provided more information about the trip to Enid, presumably in association with Mr. Weasner. After returning from Wichita on the morning of April 20, investigators interviewed Edna, Grace, and Ralph's nephew, Robert McCrory of Sterling in Newton. During the interview, Grace produced a letter she had received from Ralph postmarked March 19, 1957. Agent Kline thought it could pertain to the investigation.

> Have a friend here in town wants me to go to Enid and Emporia. It would be an overnight trip to either place. Visit an old friend in Enid.

Edna showed investigators a postcard Ralph had written to her. It was dated April 6, 1957, ten days before he went to Newton at Mr. Weasner's request.

> Went to Enid Monday and back Tuesday. Visited a little with Forest [Forrest] Cameron.

Forrest Cameron was a farmer and, at one time, had employed Ralph.

Long Time Dead

As noted in a supplementary report by Agent Kline dated April 25, Sheriff Morford had received a telephone call from Edna. She told him that, when Ralph lived in the Stackman Apartments on North Main several years previously, he mentioned having a friend by the name of Weasner. The only thing she remembered about Mr. Weasner was that he worked in the packing house and stuttered a lot. There is no mention in any record of Mr. Weasner's first name.

On April 22, the *Evening Kansan-Republican* newspaper reported there was no one by the name of Weasner in Newton and police were now of the opinion the reference was to a Wichita resident. The day before an article in the *Wichita Beacon* quoted Sheriff Morford as saying that four families with names similar to Weasner lived in Harvey County, where Newton is located, and they were being contacted. Apparently, the sheriff's investigation proved fruitless.

In the same issue of the newspaper, Mrs. Girvin is reported as saying she had informed Sheriff Morford about an incident in late February or early March that had greatly upset Ralph. A man whom he had met at a neighbourhood grocery store had asked Ralph to sign his brother's name to a note. The type of note, financial or otherwise, is not specified. Mrs. Girvin did not say if Ralph had mentioned knowing the man before the encounter. The request was made while the man gave Ralph a ride home from the store. According to the article, police officers were investigating Mrs. Girvin's report. This was the only mention of the incident.

While at the Girvin residence, the officers checked Ralph's apartment. They found the book *How to Live 100*

Wichita

Years and records of accounts in five financial institutions. He had a checking account, #7494, with the amount of $376.51 at the First National Bank in Wichita. He also had investment accounts in four institutions: Thomas Investment Co., United Building & Loan Co., and Empire Trust Co. in Wichita, and United Funds in Kansas City, Missouri. Agent Kline reported that all these accounts were checked on April 22, and none showed a recent withdrawal of any size. He did not mention the amount of funds in each of the four investment accounts. No other information of consequence was obtained according to Agent Kline.

Four investment accounts seem a lot for a man who supposedly did not have much money. The accounts could have been opened at various times, and some or all of them may have become dormant. Noted for being frugal, did Ralph accumulate considerable savings from his meager salaries? On the other hand, did the number of accounts suggest Ralph had an unknown source of money, perhaps related to his murder? Why did Ralph have an account at an institution located in Kansas City, Missouri, a city with which he had little if any connection?

There seems to be only two occasions when Ralph had received comparable large amounts of money. One was when he was discharged from the army in 1919 and paid $6,637.12. Sterling was his primary place of residence for years after the war, so it seems reasonable to assume he would have deposited the money in a financial institution there or in Hutchinson, the closest large city. The funds may have been spent or transferred to an institution in another city later.

Long Time Dead

In 1943, Ralph received $3,125 from the sale of the property he had inherited from his father. At the time, he was living in Wichita, so he would likely have deposited the funds in an institution there.

No records have been found about what happened to the accounts at financial institutions or anything about the disposition of their contents. There is no evidence of a will Ralph may have left.

During the interview with family members on April 20, officers learned that Grace and Edna and Edna's husband, Charles, had planned to meet Ralph at a clothing store in Wichita on Thursday evening, April 18. The store remained open until 9:00 p.m. Plans were changed, however, because of a church event in Hutchinson. The letter Edna sent explaining the change arrived on Thursday morning, two days after Ralph had gone to Newton at Mr. Weasner's request.

The apparent purpose of the meeting was for Ralph's sisters and brother-in-law to buy him clothes. A bachelor, he may have appreciated assistance in selecting clothes. Regardless of the reason, it seems reasonable that a man of Ralph's character would have done his best to keep the appointment.

For several days following Ralph's death, investigators interviewed friends and acquaintances he had known prior to his residency at the Girvin home. Mrs. Joyce E. Meyers said Ralph had lived on the third floor of the Stackman Apartments on North Main Street the entire time of her management there from 1951 to 1954. She remembered Ralph as being a model tenant who had few friends. The only exception was Arlie Decker, who worked at the Riley Lumber Company as a labourer and was originally from

Wichita

Halstead, Kansas. Ralph told Mrs. Meyers that he had gone home with Mr. Decker a time or two. Mr. Decker was 27 years old at the time, according to Mrs. Meyers, while Ralph would have been in his 60s.

Agent Kline reported Mrs. Meyers as saying:

> Decker was an odd ball.
>
> He worked at Riley Lumber Company as a labourer.
>
> Snair had told her that Decker wrote a lot of letters to matrimonial agencies and had a lot of dirty pictures in his room. This amused Snair.
>
> She stated that she had seen Snair and Decker together since Snair moved.
>
> Decker committed suicide about a year ago.
>
> Snair said he was going to see Decker's folks at Halstead.

Mrs. Meyers recalled that Ralph was in good health at the time and did not impress her as being deeply religious. The last time she had seen Ralph, about September 1956, less than a year before he was murdered, he said he was going to get married.

Long Time Dead

Agent Kline also interviewed Mr. George Lassley, who lived at the Stackman Apartments the same time as Ralph. Mr. Lassley said he hardly knew Ralph because he worked nights, slept days, and had little opportunity to become acquainted.

On April 24, Agent Kline interviewed Mrs. Hester Hawkins, who currently managed the rental property of the Steinbushel Estate, which included the Stackman Apartments. She had been in the same position for a number of years. Mrs. Hawkins knew Ralph, describing him as did his other acquaintances—a quiet, nice fellow.

She turned over the cash receipt book of the Stackman Apartments, which covered the period from January 1, 1952 to March 13, 1954, when they closed. She stated that she had burned the register, but the receipt book had all the last names of the registrants for that period. Ralph checked out on March 9, 1954, four days before the apartments closed. It seems likely he moved directly to the Girvin residence.

Mrs. Hawkins suggested Agent Kline contact Mrs. Mickey Steele, who had managed the Stackman Apartments for the last 18 months of its existence, and Reverend Champey of the Broadway Christian Church. There was no evidence that either person was ever interviewed.

Agents Kline and Lansdowne spoke with A. A. Way of North Chautauqua Avenue in Wichita. He was the former custodian at the College Hill Methodist Church whom Mrs. Girvin mentioned as possibly knowing Ralph better than anyone. Mr. Way did not provide any helpful information.

Unaccounted Time

Ralph's activities from the time he left the note for his land lady midday Tuesday, April 16, until he was murdered in the early hours of Friday, April 19, are at the core of the mystery surrounding this case. The scant written records coupled with analysis of known information leads to reasonable suggestions of where he may have gone and what he may have done during those two and a half days. Nothing is known with certainty more than 60 years after his death, but a careful look at his activities may give some insight into what led to his death.

In the note to Mrs. Girvin, Ralph said he had received a call from Mr. Weasner asking him to come to Newton and help him. Ralph writing "Mr. Weasner" rather than "a Mr. Weasner" or any qualifiers, such as "my friend Mr. Weasner," implies that Mrs. Girvin may have known of Mr. Weasner. Ralph did not say what type of help Mr. Weasner wanted and wrote that if he did not return the next day, Wednesday, April 17, he would be back on Thursday, April 18. He clearly had every intention of keeping the appointment with his sisters and brother-in-law at a clothing store on Thursday evening.

In the initial part of their investigation, Sheriff Morford and colleagues checked every room for rent in Newton. The *Evening Kansan-Republican*, April 25, 1957, reported that their search finally met with success when they spoke with Mrs. Mabel Vandervoort, manager of the Cozy Rooms at 425 1/2 Main Street. Mrs. Vandervoort identified Ralph from the photograph investigators showed her and produced the register with the signature of R. W. Snair in Ralph's handwriting.

Building with boarded windows formerly housing Cozy Rooms.

Unaccounted Time

Ralph had registered at 12:30 a.m. on the morning of Wednesday, April 17. Mrs. Vandervoort said Ralph was alone and told her he had to be at the Santa Fe Depot at 5:30 a.m. The depot was directly across the street from the Cozy Rooms. After registering, Ralph left the building for a few minutes and upon returning went directly to his room. He left the Cozy Rooms at 4:30 a.m. Mrs. Vandervoort said she knew nothing of his activities after that.

Sheriff Morford thought Ralph most likely would have returned to Wichita on a bus that left Newton southbound for Wichita at 5:45 a.m. Ralph had travelled by train or bus to Newton on the previous afternoon or evening. Sheriff Morford and colleagues uncovered evidence that Ralph had taken a taxicab from the depot to a Newton address at 8:40 p.m. on Tuesday evening. He returned from the same address to the depot about midnight, which corresponds with his 12:30 a.m. check-in time at the Cozy Rooms. In the few minutes he left the Cozy Rooms after registering, he most likely paid the waiting taxicab driver.

Mrs. Girvin said Ralph left the Chautauqua Street house in Wichita sometime between 10:30 a.m. and 2:15 p.m. on Tuesday, April 16. What did Ralph do between the time he left his residence and the 8:40 p.m. taxicab ride in Newton? The elapsed time could have varied from about six to ten hours, depending on exactly when he left Chautauqua Street. The time the bus or train departed from Wichita and length of time of the trip would account for some, perhaps much, of the time. The distance between Wichita to Newton is about 27 miles, which on today's highways is a 30-minute drive. Depending on the number of stops, if any, and their length, the trip by bus or train would have taken no more than one to two hours. What did Ralph do in the hours he spent waiting? Read newspapers? People watch? Pick up something to take to Newton?

Mrs. Girvin said Ralph did not go to his apartment after returning from Newton. The first record of his activities on Wednesday, April 17, was when he rented a car in Wichita and drove away at 2:59 p.m. That leaves about six to eight hours from the time he returned to Wichita until he rented the car.

When he paid the $20 deposit for the car, he told the attendant he was going to Emporia. In a postcard to Grace dated March 19, 1957, Ralph said he had a friend in town (Wichita) who wanted him to go to Enid and Emporia and that it would be an overnight trip to each place. On a card postmarked April 6, he wrote to Edna that he had gone to Enid and visited an old friend. Both sisters said their brother did not like to drive and did not own a car. Regardless, he must have had a driver's licence because he was able to rent a car.

Ralph told Mrs. Girvin that he wanted to drive to Enid because he would be bringing back something that was too heavy to carry on a bus or train. This is a strange comment, as both bus and train have ample cargo space. It is difficult to imagine something too heavy for a bus or train that could be transported in a car. It is easy to imagine it may have been contraband.

Was the same true for the trip he took starting April 17? It seems strange that a man noted for being frugal was willing to pay to rent a car twice within a span of three weeks. Was someone giving Ralph money? And if so, for what reason?

Unaccounted Time

Perhaps he saved the two receipts for gasoline found in the car's glove compartment so he could be reimbursed.

Those two receipts and the odometer readings give what limited insights we have as to where Ralph went from Wednesday afternoon in Wichita to Friday in the Walton area where he was found dead at the side of the road. These facts, coupled with Sheriff Morford's estimate that the rented car could travel 15 miles on a gallon of gasoline, give some idea where Ralph could have gone. The 17-gallon gasoline tank was full when he rented the car.

One of the gas receipts was from the Mecca Service Station in Augusta, Kansas. Augusta is 21 miles east of Wichita. Agent Lansdowne went to the station and spoke with the manager, B.F. Smooth, who remembered Ralph had been alone and had purchased gasoline at approximately 6:30 a.m. on the morning of April 18. He could not recall anything out of the ordinary about Ralph.

In his report of Agent Lansdowne's visit to Augusta, Agent Kline wrote the amount of gasoline purchased was five gallons. Earlier, he stated the amount was three gallons. The two-gallon difference may have been an error made by the typist working with Kline's handwritten material. The receipt was in Sheriff Morford's possession and is no longer available. From all other information, including newspaper reports, it seems likely the five-gallon amount is correct. This discrepancy of two gallons is significant because it equates to an additional 30 miles Ralph could have travelled.

Where could Ralph have gone on five gallons of gas and what did he do when he was not driving? Sixteen and a half hours had elapsed from the time he rented the car on April 17 until he purchased gasoline on the morning of April 18. Estimating 15 miles per gallon, Ralph would have driven about 75 miles. He could have driven to Newton, returned to Wichita, and then gone to Augusta for a total of 75 miles. Another route would have been to go to Newton and directly from Newton to Augusta for a total of 72 miles.

The second gas receipt was for the purchase of 10.1 gallons of regular gasoline (ticket #2344) at the Kurtz "66" Service Station in Florence. Agent Kline went to Florence and spoke with the young station attendant, who said Ralph was alone when he filled up with gasoline on the evening of April 18. This indicates he drove about 150 miles after filling up that morning in Augusta. The distance from Augusta to Emporia is 74 miles and from Emporia to the where the car was found outside of Walton about 64 miles for a total of 138 miles. Considering he may have driven around Emporia and accounting for a margin of error in the calculations presented here, the difference between 138 and 150 miles could be insignificant.

It required four and a half gallons to fill the gas tank after the car was taken by the Nordstrom-Smuck Ford Agency nine miles from the death scene to Newton. Assuming the car was towed, then it had been driven about 67 miles after the fill up in Florence. But the distance between Florence and the scene is only 20 miles. How to account for the 47-mile difference between the one and one-third gallons of gasoline needed to cover 20 miles and the four and a half gallons used?

Ralph could have met his killer(s) somewhere in those 47 miles. The gas station attendant in Florence said Ralph

Unaccounted Time

was alone. Had a rendezvous somewhere between Florence and the scene been pre-arranged?

When the car was found, the odometer reading was 23,790 miles, 308 miles more than when Ralph left the rental agency in Wichita. This difference of 308 miles equates approximately to the distance that he could have travelled on the total 19.6 gallons of gasoline he purchased. A possible explanation is that he drove from Wichita to Newton on the afternoon of April 17, picked up something, and spent the night, perhaps with the person he had visited the evening before. On April 18, he drove to Augusta and then to Emporia, where he met someone and delivered the item he got in Newton. He could have then taken that item or another item from Emporia to someplace between Florence and Walton. There he met the recipient(s) of the item who were involved in his murder.

Sheriff Morford and colleagues scoured the area from Wichita to Augusta to Emporia to Walton for any trace of Ralph. After examining Ralph's photograph, several people said they may have seen Ralph, but no one was able to give any details. The sheriff spent a day and a half in Emporia, checking all the rooming houses, hotels, and motels and all other likely places Ralph may have stayed. He did not find anything.

According to the five gallons of gasoline Ralph purchased in Augusta on Thursday morning, April 18, he could not have travelled to or near Emporia and spent the previous night, April 17, there. It was also impossible for Ralph to have spent Thursday night, April 18, in Emporia. He bought gas in Florence Thursday evening and was shot in the early hours of Friday, April 19. The coroner wrote that Ralph "could have been killed as early as 1:30 a.m. on the 19th." Bread delivery man Kenneth Armstrong saw the car containing Ralph's body parked at the side of the road at 4:30 a.m.

The Trip to Enid

At 8:00 a.m. on March 29, 1957, Ralph rented a green, four-door Chevrolet from the U-Drive-It car rental agency in Wichita. This was the same agency where he rented the Ford in which he would be found dead three weeks later. Agency manager Mr. David Stavniak said Ralph had told him on March 29 that he was going to Oklahoma City. When Ralph returned the next day, the Chevrolet's odometer showed a total of 235 miles had been driven. Mr. Stavniak told Ralph this was not enough miles for him to have gone to Oklahoma City. There is no record of Ralph's reply, if any. The distance of a return trip from Wichita to Oklahoma City is 325 miles. The 235 miles Ralph drove, however, is close to the number of miles required for a return trip from Wichita to Enid, and in fact, he did drive to Enid, apparently by himself. In 1957, the City of Enid, which lies to the southwest of Wichita, had about 37,000 inhabitants.

The information about Ralph's trip to Enid supplied by the Girvins, Edna, Grace, and Mr. Stavniak elicited considerable interest from investigators. On April 23, Agent Lansdowne drove to Enid and met with Chief of Police

Long Time Dead

Dale Moxley and Detective H. E. Henderson. Together, they contacted Forrest Cameron, whom Ralph had visited on March 29. Mr. Cameron said Ralph had worked for him for about a year in 1945. He then worked as a farmhand for C. H. Cole and Al Holland, who had a farm a short distance from the Cameron place. Both Mr. Cole and Mr. Holland were former bootleggers.

Mr. Cameron said Ralph, who was alone and driving a green Chevrolet, arrived about 1:30 p.m. and left two hours later. He recalled Ralph saying the car belonged to his boss, who was also his landlord, and that he had driven the car to Enid while his landlord had driven a truck loaded with auto parts to sell there. Ralph was to meet his boss in front of the Enid Court House, and as soon as they could dispose of the truck and parts, they would return to Wichita.

Investigators found that Ralph had checked into the Newton Hotel in Enid at approximately 11:00 p.m. on March 29 and left the following morning. He was alone. They could not find any evidence that Ralph's landlord, Garrett Girvin, had stayed at any hotel in Enid.

Agent Lansdowne wrote:

> Up to this time it looked to us as if Snair
> was lying for some reason or other, reason
> known only to him.

Immediately following this statement, Lansdowne wrote:

> Many hours were spent in trying to find
> a close associate of Snair's but to no avail.

The Trip to Enid

> Many leads were run out and so far it seems to be just the process of elimination.

Agent Lansdowne does not explicitly say whether or not the "close associate" he mentioned in his report was connected to the trip to Enid. Could the associate have been Mr. Weasner?

On April 24, Detective Howard E. Richardson wrote to Agent Lansdowne:

> In regards to G.A. Girvin of your city, I found out this date that he was in Enid, Oklahoma approx. three weeks ago and called on The Motor Supply Co., North Independence Street, Mr. McClellan the manager & has been calling on them for 20 years representing The C.E. Nichoff & Co. out of Chicago, Ill. He does not sell merchandise from his car and does not take orders as they order direct from the factory.

Agent Lansdowne wrote:

> Mr. McClellan stated that Mr. Girvin travels the whole state of Texas & Oklahoma. Also this date he was in Enid, Okla., and called on the Silver's Electric Inc. on West Cherokee Street.

> Have checked all motels and hotels and fail to find him registered on the 29th day of March.

Mr. Girvin was presumably involved in the promotion of Nichoff merchandise, that is, providing information about new equipment, not sales.

The above account taken from the KBI file casts suspicion on the reason Ralph went to Enid. This suspicion rests primarily on Mr. Cameron recalling Ralph had said the green Chevrolet belonged to his boss who was also his landlord. The word landlord brings Garrett Girvin into the story. But what if Mr. Cameron did not remember correctly after the elapse of a month? It is not an unusual occurrence to mix up people in someone else's story. It happens every day in countless conversations.

What if the man to whom Ralph referred was indeed Mr. Weasner? He could have been involved in the transport of auto parts for whatever reason and paid Ralph for his services and the cost of renting the car. Ralph may well have used the term "boss" for him. If Mr. Weasner was present in Enid, he did not stay with Ralph the night of March 29. Investigators found that Ralph had been alone.

Ralph made no secret of his trip to Enid. He had spoken to Mrs. Girvin of his plans. Previously, he had told his sister Grace in a card dated March 19 that he had a friend in town who wanted him to go to Enid and Emporia. This date was shortly after Ralph would have met up again with his friend from North Main, most likely Mr. Weasner. On April 6,

The Trip to Enid

Ralph wrote to his sister Edna that he had gone to Enid and visited an old friend.

The trip itself would not necessarily be suspicious, except that Ralph apparently gave contradictory information, perhaps intentionally—first to the manager of the car rental agency and then to Forrest Cameron—strange behaviour for a man reputed to be of such upstanding character. Ralph's trip to Enid, his comments about his destination, and mention of his landlord are the first in a series of unusual events that end with his death.

The Gun

The bullet that ended Ralph's life was shot from a .22 calibre sealed eight-shot Iver Johnson revolver, model 68, made of blue steel and with a wooden grip. Firearms—pistols, revolvers, and rifles—of this calibre are extremely common, readily acquired, and inexpensive. The ammunition is abundant and nearly impossible to trace. The revolvers are easy to use, carry, and conceal. They are effective killing machines. A .22 shot to the head is as deadly as a 9 mm and much quieter. A .22 bullet has enough kinetic energy to enter the skull and cause extensive damage to the brain, but not enough to exit. There is little bleeding. These features—small entry hole, damaged brain, no exit wound, and little blood—are consistent with the reports of investigators and of the pathologist who performed the autopsy. The most famous killing with such a firearm occurred on June 5, 1968, when Sirhan Sirhan shot presidential candidate Robert Kennedy with an eight-shot Iver Johnson .22 calibre revolver.

Upon careful examination of the gun, experts at the Wichita Police Department confirmed its description, reported on the contents of the chambers, and noted the

The Gun

lack of fingerprints. They also checked Ralph's hands for gunshot residue. KBI investigators delved into the history of the gun's ownership, which, despite considerable effort, resulted in more questions than answers.

The WPD made a puzzling discovery about the contents of the murder weapon's cylinder. As would be expected, the police found the spent cartridge that killed Ralph to be under the hammer. This spent cartridge was followed to the left in turn by two spent (fired) cartridges, three live cartridges, an empty chamber, and lastly a live cartridge. Did the person who fired the gun know the next two chambers contained spent cartridges and that one chamber was empty? What happened to the two spent cartridges? Had the empty chamber recently contained a bullet? The *Wichita Beacon*, April 21, 1957, reported that no bullet holes were found in the car.

Long Time Dead

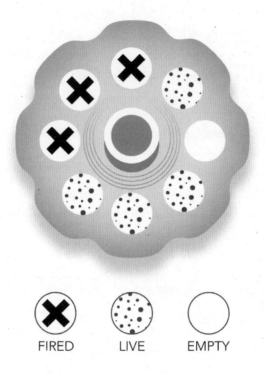

Diagram of cylinder of revolver. Cylinder rotates to right, clockwise. X-fired, stippled-live, blank-empty chamber.

The Wichita police found the gun had been wiped clean of fingerprints, as Sheriff Morford had thought and as Coroner Martin reported. Police believed the white linen handkerchief found on the front seat beside Ralph had been used to wipe away fingerprints. The lack of prints almost certainly negates the possibility that Ralph had used the gun to commit suicide; it is exceedingly difficult for a dead man to remove fingerprints! However, he could possibly

The Gun

have held the gun with the handkerchief while pulling the trigger, preventing any trace of his fingerprints.

The initial examination of the gun surface would likely have been done by Harvey County authorities at the nighttime scene. In the darkness, the interior car light, flashlights, and perhaps other accessory lighting would have been the sources of illumination. The gun may also have been examined later in Newton before being taken to Wichita. These superficial examinations would have most likely been able to detect only patent prints—that is, prints that are made by someone with substances, such as ink, grease, or blood on their fingers. Patent prints are readily visible to the naked eye. Latent prints, the most common type, occur when someone touches a surface, such as the handle or barrel of a gun. They are usually detected by dusting the surface with powder, which adheres to the residue deposited by fingers. Care must be taken not to smudge any existing print.

There is no mention of examination of the live or spent cartridges in the cylinder for fingerprints. Such information could have helped to identify the person who placed the shells into the revolver.

The paraffin technique, also known as the dermal nitrate test, was used to determine if there was gunshot residue on Ralph's hands, indicating that he had fired the revolver. This technique consists of spraying or pouring hot liquid paraffin over the fingers, hands, and wrists until a coating of paraffin is built up. Successive layers of cotton or other fabric are added with additional paraffin until a paraffin glove is finally moulded. When cooled, the glove is peeled from the hand, and diphenylamine in a concentrated solution of sulfuric acid is added to the paraffin glove drop by drop. The appearance of dark blue pin-point specks on the inner surface of the cast indicates the presence of gunshot residues. The paraffin casts were made in Newton and the results analyzed by Wichita experts.

Coroner Martin wrote:

> The report was returned "negative," meaning that the test did not show that the victim had fired the gun, however, a negative test is regarded as inconclusive.

The reliability of the paraffin test, as Coroner Martin noted, is indeed questionable. False negatives are known to occur even in situations where it has been conclusively demonstrated that a person had fired the gun shortly before the paraffin glove was made. These false results can occur if a revolver is well made and in good condition so that the space between the cylinder and the entrance to the gun barrel are at a minimum. This situation would result in the escape of a negligible amount of gas. On the contrary, false positives can result if the person has had recent contact with other substances containing nitrates, for example, bleaching agents, explosives, and fertilizers.

The lack of fingerprints and of gunshot residue evidence made the question of the ownership of the gun especially important. On May 14, 1957, agents Kline and Lansdowne filed a supplementary report on the murder weapon, which detailed the sequence of ownership as follows: On July 16, 1951 the manufacturer, Iver Johnson Arms Co., Fitchburg,

The Gun

Mass sent the pistol to W & K Wholesale Distributor in Fort Worth, Texas. On July 24, 1951, Stewart Tracy of Midland, Texas purchased it. At some date marked 'unknown' in the K.B.I. report, Tracy sold the gun to DeHart's Pawn Shop in Odessa, Texas.

A front-page story of the *Evening Kansan-Republican* dated April 29, 1957, said the gun had been traced to a travelling salesman living in Midland, Texas, presumably Stewart Tracy. In the newspaper account investigators were trying to get in touch with the salesman for further history of the pistol. No additional information about Mr. Tracy was found. Interestingly, another travelling salesman, Ralph Howell Campbell, was among those individuals whom investigators suspected of murdering Ralph.

On October 4, 1951, Cecil Dumas of El Paso, Texas, purchased the weapon from the DeHart's pawn shop. Agent Kline requested the director of the KBI, Logan H. Sanford, contact the Texas Rangers for assistance in locating Dumas. A week later, Gully Cowbert, Captain, Co. "E", Texas Rangers wrote to Director Sanford:

> We have made a thorough search for all the El Paso records, checked the pawn shops, city and criminal records and have been unable to locate any one [*sic*] using the name Dumas, except one Ed Dumas, whose last known place of residence was in El Paso, Texas.

> On further check we found that this man, Ed Dumas, had been dead for approximately three years & that an attorney, Volney Brown, was handling the Ed Dumas Estate. Contacted Mr. Brown who had a list of all known relatives of Ed Dumas, deceased, but the name of Cecil Dumas did not appear on this list. We will continue making a further check on the above, but it is my opinion that Cecil Dumas has not lived in El Paso here in the past ten years.

Agent Kline wrote to Roland on August 27, 1957, that his trip to Texas to identify Cecil Dumas had been unsuccessful. He concluded:

> The only thing which will establish positively what happened will be ownership of the gun. Thus far we haven't had much result on this count.

It is a mystery what happened to the gun from October 4, 1951, until its appearance at the death scene on April 19, 1957. The police were unable to trace its ownership during that time because the gun apparently had gone "underground"—that is, transfer from one person to another was not registered. The gun may have had multiple owners and may have been stolen at some point. Whatever the gun's

The Gun

history, it was used to kill Ralph, and his murderer knew it could not be traced.

The age of the gun and its checkered history with multiple owners suggest it was not in top condition. This substantiates the validity of the negative results for gunshot residue on Ralph's hand and that he did not fire the gun himself. False negatives usually occur only when a revolver is in good condition.

PART II

Autopsy

Death marks the end of the physical body, but the body tells the story of its works and days at autopsy; sometimes a whole biography is there in the cast and color of the blood and bone, the wounds and scars gathered over a lifetime.

Unnatural Death: Confessions of a Medical Examiner. p. 33. 1989. M. M. Baden and J. A. Hennessee. Ivy Books, New York. 223 pp.

Answers and Questions

The day after the discovery of Ralph's body, Dr. K. M. Neudorfer performed an autopsy at Saint Francis Hospital in Wichita. The results confirmed the cause of death and answered some questions while raising others. This chapter and the subsequent chapters in Part II present Dr. Neudorfer's findings along with related information I uncovered in my investigation.

Note: Dr. Neudorfer used the metric system for some measurements and the imperial system for others. He described the body as that of a well-developed, well-nourished white male measuring six feet in length and weighing approximately 160 pounds. The body appeared to be that a man of the stated age of 67. The hair was short and grey. The head was balding, especially on top, and the hairline receding on both sides of the temporal region. This description matched how I remember Ralph.

The cause of death was confirmed as a single gunshot to the right side of the head. The point of entry of the fatal bullet was a small round wound in the skin of the scalp, situated in the right parietal area eight centimetres above the anterior edge of

Answers and Questions

the right ear. Within the lacerated brain tissue in the parietal area, Dr. Neudorfer observed two tiny irregular fragments of lead and several small bone chips. He found a large piece of the bullet on the left side in the temporal area. On the inner aspects of the bone covering the temporal area, there was a small star-shaped fracture but no external fracture. Dr. Neudorfer did not mention an exit wound.

Some investigators had speculated that Ralph had been shot elsewhere and the body transported to the site of discovery on Highway 50, while others thought death occurred at the scene. After careful reading of the autopsy report, relying on my experience as a coroner, and consulting with Jeff Everden, a funeral home director with whom I had worked, I concluded that Ralph was shot at the scene. My conclusion is based on the process of lividity, also known as liver mortis, which occurs when the blood pools in response to gravity after the heart stops beating. The location of the pooled blood indicates the position of the person at the time of death and enables investigators to determine if a body has been moved.

Dr. Neudorfer reported:

> a bluish-red patchy discoloration of the skin of the left chest, of the skin of the left lateral abdominal wall of the left flank of the anterior wall and part of the anterior wall of the left chest

The patchy discolouration was in all probability caused by lividity, which had faded due to embalming having been performed prior to autopsy. According to records, Forrest V. Daly performed arterial embalming at the funeral home in Newton before the body was transported to Wichita. The different locations of the embalmer (Newton) and the pathologist (Wichita) was probably the reason for reversing the usual sequence of the two procedures. Customarily, the autopsy is done first to eliminate any alterations of the body due to replacing the blood with embalming fluid. This procedure can cause areas of the skin to appear lighter in colour than it would have been when blood was present. This can be of particular significance in criminal cases. Ralph's body was found leaning to the left in the car, which corresponds with Dr. Neudorfer's observations.

The question remains whether Ralph was seated in the middle of the front seat when shot or behind the steering wheel and pulled to the middle so that his body would slump to the left below the line of sight of anyone passing by. Coroner Martin raised this possibility when he wrote:

> It is not known whether he was actually sitting in that position (right of the middle of the front seat) or was placed in that fashion to allow space for his head to rest against the left door.

It is conceivable that Ralph had been driving, stopped the vehicle for some reason, and was then shot by a passenger, who pulled the body to the middle of the seat. The lividity pattern would be the same regardless of where Ralph was sitting when shot.

Answers and Questions

Dr. Neudorfer also reported:

> No other wounds can be identified on the head or anyplace else on the body.

The lack of readily identifiable cuts or bruises or other relevant evidence on the hands and arms indicate that Ralph had not tried to defend himself. This is consistent with investigators not finding evidence that a struggle had occurred in the car or of any disturbance in the area around the car. However, Dr. Neudorfer did describe small abrasions on the scalp, which may have lost much of their original colouration because the body had been embalmed before autopsy. During my investigation, I asked a physician, Dr. Khati Hendry, to review the autopsy report. She said the abrasions suggest that Ralph may have been "roughed up" prior to death. Four of the five somewhat oval shaped or elongated abrasions were located at the vertex (top) of the head. The largest measured 3 centimetres in length and 1.5 centimetres at greatest width. A similar larger area measuring 4 centimetres in length and 1.5 centimetres in width was present in the occipital area at the lower back of the head.

I found it particularly interesting that the occipital bone beneath the abrasion in the occipital area was fractured while there was not any internal damage observed in the underlying (occipital) part of the brain. In contrast, the areas of the brain covered by bones that were fractured by the impact of the gunshot—frontal, right temporal, and right and left parietal—showed extensive damage. The lack of damage to the occipital region of the brain lends support to the possibility that the fracture of the overlying bone resulted from a blow to the back of the head. An alternative explanation is the fracture was caused by internal pressure generated within the rigid skull by the gunshot. While it is tempting to conclude that Ralph had been struck repeatedly, perhaps even pistol whipped, it cannot be discounted that the abrasions were caused by other activities.

Distinct from the abrasions, a small area of edema (swelling) and dark bluish discolouration was found within the skin of the outer angle of the left eye. The swollen area extended into the outer portion of the left upper eyelid and measured 4 centimetres long and 1.5 centimetres wide. The edema and discolouration were probably caused by Ralph's head striking the arm rest on the driver's side door. In photographs taken at the scene, Ralph's glasses are seen to be in their usual position, not particularly askew. The left side of the glasses could have been compressed upon impact with the arm rest, causing the swelling and discolouration reported by Dr. Neudorfer. There is the possibility, however, that he had been struck by an assailant.

In his detailed examination, Dr. Neudorfer found fibrous scaring at the apices of the lungs, a result of Ralph having been gassed in the First World War. He also reported conditions, such as arteriosclerosis, consistent with Ralph's age and various anatomic and microscopic conditions and anomalies, not related to the cause of death.

A Correction and Its Implication

The autopsy report substantiated information I had received months earlier from the KBI concerning a statement made by the sheriff that had misled the family for years. At the gathering of cousins in Hutchinson in summer 2017, we never questioned whether or not Ralph had been murdered. After all, we had been told by older family members that Ralph had died at the hands of another person, and we even had a copy of a news article to prove it.

Wichita Beacon reporter Bill Hazlett wrote in his article of April 21, 1957:

> Morford said the bullet entered Snair's head from above and behind the right ear, "in such a way that it would have been almost impossible for him to have shot himself, unless he turned the pistol upside down."

Long Time Dead

This is a direct quote from Sheriff Morford, not the reporter's interpretation of what he said. I clearly remember Sue at the cousin reunion trying to manoeuvre her hand and arm into the awkward position Ralph would have had to assume to shoot himself while holding the pistol upside down.

Although a written record does not exist of the meeting between Sheriff Morford and Ralph's two sisters and nephew on April 20, the day after discovery of Ralph's body and the day before publication of Hazlett's article, he must have told them the same information. And so, for over 60 years the family, apart from Ralph's brother Roland, never questioned that it was impossible for Ralph to have committed suicide.

Much to my surprise, I read in the letter of March 15, 2018, from Ms. Laura Graham, counsel of the KBI:

> Your November 9, 2017 letter to us mentioned your understanding that Mr. Snair had been "shot in the back of the head." The April 19, 1957 report by Agents Kline and Lansdowne indicated the following: "Cause of Death: Gunshot wound – 2 1/4" above and 1" to the front of the center of top of right ear."

Although I thought the agents' statement was probably correct, I wanted definitive proof and only the autopsy report could provide it. My hope that the report would eventually turn up was realized in September 2018, when I received a copy of the autopsy report from the Harvey

A Correction and Its Implication

County Coroner's Office. It confirmed the information in Ms. Graham's letter.

> There is a small round wound in the skin of the scalp in the right parietal area measuring 7 mm. in diameter. The wound is situated 8 cm. just above the anterior edge of the right ear. The edge of the wound is irregular and somewhat lacerated.

In other words, Ralph could have shot himself. Although the consensus was that Ralph had been murdered, the possibility of suicide could not be ruled out solely based on the location of the entry site of the fatal bullet.

Why Sheriff Morford gave the press and the family incorrect information is not known. He had seen the body at the scene. The photographs taken at the time of discovery of Ralph's body clearly show the site of the entry wound to be at the side, not the back, of the head. Also, the sheriff apparently had not spoken with Dr. Neudorfer, who performed the autopsy within about 18 hours after discovery of Ralph's body. For the sheriff to make a statement about what he thought was the exact location of the gunshot was unwise. It certainly contravenes the accepted practice of modern law enforcement officers to rely on experts for such information.

Was the sheriff trying to protect the family against what he thought they would have considered the disgrace of suicide? Did he realize he was knowingly altering a basic premise of the case? If so, he forgot the well-known fact that the truth will come out, even six decades later.

Perhaps, he did not accurately remember, or he was sloppy in his work. The site of the fatal wound is not the only incorrect statement Sheriff Morford was reported to have made. He told Hazlett that Ralph was slumped forward in the front seat of the car rather than falling to his left and coming to rest on the arm rest of the driver's side door. Hazlett did not include this information as a direct quote. Sheriff Morford also said the car key was attached to Ralph's belt, whereas it was a Yale key to Ralph's apartment as identified by the coroner.

From the KBI file, it appears Sheriff Morford was diligent in investigating Ralph's case; however, he may not have been well trained for police work. He had worked for the Santa Fe Railroad before he was elected sheriff in 1955, and again in 1957. After his second term, he moved to Florida, where he was employed by General Electric of Cape Canaveral. He then transferred to Daytona Beach with the same company and worked on the development of fighter jets. Whatever Morford's level of competency as a sheriff, he was not a career law enforcement officer and gave incorrect and misleading information to the press and family.

In contrast, his brother, Galen Morford, was elected sheriff of Harvey County in 1973 and served in that capacity until his retirement in 1990. Previously, he had been a Newton city police officer for 23 years. During his four decades in law enforcement, he received many awards and certificates for his work.

Suicide Revisited

Not only did I discover in Ms. Graham's letter of March 15, 2018, that it was physically possible for Ralph to have shot himself, I also learned that his brother Roland had raised the question of suicide and that KBI investigators had already been considering the possibility. Results of the autopsy did not support one of the reasons for suicide Roland mentioned. Ms. Graham appended photocopies of correspondence between Roland and Agent Kline to her letter. Below are extracts of those letters and my comments.

In his letter of August 24, 1957 to Agent Kline, Roland wrote:

> I am sure you have done all you possibly can in trying to solve this tragedy. My two sisters, Edna Wilson of Hutchinson & Grace Currie of Sterling have had nothing but praise for what you have done.
>
> I have always thought that this was foul play by someone. But since no trace of the

criminal has ever been found and 4 long months has [*sic*] passed, I am beginning to look at it from another angle. And this angle is that Ralph could have taken his own life. Now I am probably wrong but I am writing this letter to you to see what you think of this angle of the case.

There are so many things that point to this angle of the case that I wanted your honest opinion. I know or knew my brother so well as he was just 2 years younger than I. In past years he and I had worked so many days together on the farm.

One of my sisters told me not long ago that Ralph said he needed an operation badly but he would never consent to it. So his health might have had something to do with his tragic end.

I always thought of Ralph as a sincere devout Christian and that is the reason that from the first, I could never believe he took his own life.

But now I am beginning to believe he could have taken his own life. The fact that he hired or rented this car [something he never did before] and was driving around

Suicide Revisited

> in it for 2 or 3 days makes me think that he was trying to decide for quite a while just where & when he would take his life.

The sister Roland referred to was probably Grace, a registered nurse and widow of a physician. In his detailed examination at autopsy, Dr. Neudorfer did not uncover any evidence of a condition that would have required an operation, such as a tumour. None of the individuals interviewed by investigators mentioned Ralph having health problems. It appears health concerns were not a factor in the unlikely event of suicide.

Roland was apparently unaware that Ralph had rented a car on March 29 for the trip to Enid, Oklahoma.

A letter prepared by Agent Kline, signed by KBI Director Logan H. Sanford, and dated August 27, 1957, was sent to Roland. Agent Kline wrote:

> Have at hand your letter of August 24, 1957 in regard to the death of your brother Ralph. It's good to hear from you and interesting to note that some thoughts have come to you that have bothered us for some time.

> It appeared in the beginning that someone had murdered Ralph and attempted to make it look like he had taken his own life. But as we weigh the meager facts of the case and analyze what we know of Ralph

> Snair, we realize that what could have happened was the opposite of what we considered in the first place. In considering a matter of this sort we must naturally mix conjecture with fact.

It seems strange to me that law enforcement personnel would send a letter mixing conjecture with fact to a family member of a murdered individual. Agent Kline says that based on an analysis of "the meager facts of the case," suicide was being considered. However, he does not say exactly what fact(s) caused the change of thought. Was the reason, as Roland suggested, simply because the homicide case had not been solved in four months?

Agent Kline continued:

> First, we should consider the type of man Ralph was. As you pointed out, he was a sincere devout Christian.
>
> He apparently thought a good deal of his brothers and sisters as they did of him. At the same time we must consider his health was very poor and that he was probably a very lonely man having much idle time in which to think about his physical condition.

Suicide Revisited

> Possibly his troubles became too great for him to handle and he saw no further need for life.

Why did Agent Kline think Ralph was in poor health? Was it Roland's letter? In the KBI file I examined, there is no mention of Ralph not being well—physically, emotionally, or psychologically. Perhaps Agent Kline did not appreciate the lack of findings in the autopsy report that would indicate the need for an operation. He had access to the report as evidenced by his stating the correct site of the gunshot in the KBI file.

Agent Kline then presented a theoretical plan Ralph may have developed to disguise suicide.

> If this was the case, he thought enough of his family to devise a plan in which he would disguise the fact that he took his own life.

> He didn't want to involve any of his associates of which he had few, so he had to create a person that he could be involved with.

> He first referred to this person by writing to his sister Grace on March 19, 1957, stating he has a friend who wanted him to go to Enid and Emporia with him and that he was going.

Long Time Dead

Then on April 6 he wrote to his other sister, Edna, stating that he had been to Enid. This was found to be true in that he had rented a car to take the trip and he had seen an old friend while there. The friend stated that Ralph came to see him alone and identified the rented car as belonging to his landlord, Mr. Girvin. [By the time Agent Kline wrote this letter, the KBI had already established that the car did not belong to Mr. Girvin.] We found the hotel that he stayed in on that night and registered in alone and was not seen with anyone.

The next we hear of this person is on April 16 when he leaves a note for his landlady, Mrs. Girvin, stating that he had received a call from a Mr. Weasner asking him to go to Newton with him. Found that he was in Newton that night. He checked in at a small hotel there after midnight alone. He stayed two or three hours and left without anyone seeing him.

The following day Apr. 17 he rented a car in Wichita alone and was not seen again until the following morning at Augusta where he bought 5 gal of gasoline. He was alone here also. That evening he purchased

Suicide Revisited

gas again at Florence sometime between 5:00 and 6:00. The attendant was not sure at this station but thought he remembered the incident and thought he was alone. It was sometime during that night of the 18th that his life was taken.

It has been established that Ralph disliked guns very much and we haven't been able to establish the current ownership of the gun.

There are simpler ways to disguise a suicide than creating a fictious person weeks before death, such as staging the loss of control of a car and hitting a concrete abutment or leaving clues that a drowning was the result of an accidental fall into a river. Also, it seems strange that someone with a well-known dislike of guns, even the sound of a gunshot, would choose to end his life using a firearm.

Agent Kline wrote:

> One small item that could connect him with the death weapon was that in his overnight bag was a .22 cal long rifle shell that was found in the gun.
>
> The gun had one empty chamber and the gun is of the type that a shell could fall out of the injection recess which could indicate that the gun could have been carried in the overnight bag.

Long Time Dead

It seems highly unusual, even unlikely, that a shell would simply fall out of a chamber as mentioned by Agent Kline. The probability of this occurring is diminished in this instance because the type of revolver used was "sealed," a safety feature that shields the shooter in the event of a ruptured case head (blow back). Unfortunately, Agent Kline does not elaborate on this point.

What led Agent Kline to say the bag was Ralph's? Could it have belonged to someone else? There is no mention of the bag either in the KBI file I examined, mostly written by Agent Kline, or in the coroner's report. If the bag was Ralph's, he likely packed it before leaving for Newton in response to the telephone call from Mr. Weasner on Tuesday, April 16. Ralph's landlady said he did not go home between the time he retuned from Newton on April 17 and rented the car that afternoon or between then and his death on April 19. Why would he have wanted a gun—for protection? To commit suicide? If the killer planted the shell to mislead investigators, he must have indeed been very clever.

By using the term "shell," I assume Agent Kline meant the bullet had been fired. The bullet that killed Ralph was followed by two bullets that had already been fired. Note that the cylinder turns to the right, clockwise. The bullets not being fired in sequence means the cylinder had been rotated, perhaps even opened, before the killing shot was fired. Where, when, and why? Russian roulette?

Did the person who fired the fatal bullet—Ralph or his killer—examine the cylinder and discover the expended bullets and their location? Although Ralph was known to dislike firearms, he was not naïve about them. He had

Suicide Revisited

served in the First World War and had used guns on the family farm. A professional killer would surely have checked his weapon before use.

Agent Kline continued:

> Another item that was somewhat unusual was that all of Ralph's pockets had been turned inside out when he was found.
>
> This is an odd thing to find at any robbery let along [*sic*] one which is to appear as a suicide.
>
> The only thing which will establish positively what happened will be the ownership of the gun. Thus far we haven't had much result on this count.

Agent Kline then wrote a brief account of what had been revealed about ownership of the gun and concluded his letter:

> Mr. Snair, I have endeavored to have set out some of the aspects of the case to you as you have requested. We cannot definitely say as to whether it was murder or suicide. If there should be further information that you may desire, please feel free to contact me.

Long Time Dead

Almost a year later June 14, 1958, Roland wrote to Agent Kline.

> I cannot bring myself to believe that Ralph took his own life although there are two or three things that point to the fact that he did.
>
> My sister Edna says that I must not even suggest the idea, but I have always had an open mind and I believe that you have to look at the tragedy from all angles.
>
> And you as an official of the Bureau have to look at it from all angles, do you NOT?

On June 25, 1958, Agent Kline replied:

> Have at hand your letter of June 14, 1958 and am sorry to report that there has been little of importance in the case of the death of your brother since my last writing.
>
> There have been some leads which we have followed up but have developed nothing of value.
>
> You first asked how long we keep a case such as this open. I might point out that

Suicide Revisited

> there is no statute of limitation in such cases as this.
>
> At the onset of a case a complete investigation is made and all leads are followed, which has been done in this case. We have gone as far as we can without further information.

Roch Fortin, a retired commissioned officer in the Royal Canadian Mounted Police with experience in murder investigations, read the investigation into Ralph's death and leans toward the possibility of suicide. A significant reason for his opinion is that the death car was found at the side of a major highway near the intersection with an unpaved country road. Mr. Fortin said that a professional would have killed Ralph and left the car some distance up the country road where there would have been less likelihood of it being seen. Other factors he considered indicative of suicide were the lack of defensive wounds on Ralph's hands and arms and Ralph's pockets having been turned inside out. "People who commit murder want to leave the scene as quickly as possible, not spend time rifling through their victims' pockets," he said.

The gun found in Ralph's lap was oriented with the handle to his right side. For the gun to be in that position, Ralph would have had to use his right hand to pull the trigger if he were right-handed, which he was. Also, Ralph was within an hour's drive of his home in Wichita when he died. As he neared the end of his journey, did the pressure from whatever source mount, causing him to act?

Long Time Dead

If Ralph had been murdered, then there was likely only one other person in the car with him and that person would have been at Ralph's right. Ralph was in the middle of the front seat, and the gunshot was to the right side of his head. Anyone sitting to his left, in the driver's seat, would have run the possibility of being struck by the exiting bullet and splattered with blood.

The following scenario explains how Ralph may have tried to make his suicide appear as a murder.

> Ralph rented a car in Wichita on the afternoon of Wednesday, April 17, and drove 308 miles. During this time, he may have been delivering goods of some sort but may have also been contemplating suicide. He intended to be away for at least one night, so he packed a bag and, at some point, acquired the gun. He possibly got the gun from a close neighbour in Wichita, a travelling perfume salesman and convicted burglar who stole many types of items including firearms (see the chapter "Ralph Howell Campbell"). In fact, the trip may have crystallized ongoing suicidal thoughts because he would be away from home. It is not uncommon for suicidal individuals to consider the impact on anyone finding the body. The trip would facilitate making the suicide look like a murder; something

Suicide Revisited

Ralph would have wanted to do out of consideration for his family.

Having completed whatever tasks, he was supposed to do on his trip and nearing home, he would have decided the time had come to act. He then parked the car at the side of the road two miles east of Walton in the early hours of April 19. Presumably, he got out of the car, walked about half the length of a football field in front of the car, and, having previously disposed of any money in the billfold, thrown it and the ignition key in the ditch. Ralph would have returned to the car and entered using the passenger side door, the door closest to the ditch and field, and sat near the middle of the bench seat.

He would have turned his pockets inside out, used his handkerchief to wipe off any fingerprints on the pistol, and wrapped the handkerchief around the grip of the pistol to prevent fingerprints. He then would have pressed the pistol to his head, turning up the brim of his hat in the process, and pulled the trigger. He fell to his left with his head coming to rest on the arm rest of the driver's side door. The pistol would have fallen into his lap and the handkerchief

> onto the seat beside him. As Agent Kline suggested, the hat, which was reported to have been found situated backwards on the right side of his head, would have turned 180 degrees due to Ralph's head striking the back of the driver's side seat during his fall to the left.

What could have been Ralph's motive? Lonely, despondent, concerned about health problems? Had he become involved in a questionable or illegal activity so deeply that it would haven difficult or impossible to extricate himself? Was he being blackmailed?

Considerable evidence points to Ralph not having any apparent indicators of someone contemplating suicide. He was engaged in life around him. He continued to work part time at the church and for the Girvins, apparently did deliveries for Mr. Weasner, and visited his friend Forest Cameron. He had a close-knit family. He interacted well with the Girvins and corresponded with his family. Ralph was scheduled to meet his sisters and brother-in-law at a clothing store on Thursday evening, April 18. He appeared in good health, abstained from alcohol, and his religious faith discouraged suicide.

Coroner Martin concluded that Ralph's death was a homicide and thought the death scene "added up to a very crude attempt to simulate suicide." After careful consideration, I agree with Coroner Martin that death was at the hands of another person. However, what appears to have been an attempt to make the scene appear as a suicide may not have been intentional.

PART III
Ralph

Not Just a Victim

An early step in my investigation was reading and rereading many times the postcards received and sent by Ralph in the album my cousin Don had assembled from several hundred family postcards saved by our great aunt Edna, Ralph's sister. Some cards were tattered, the postmarks obscured, and the handwriting difficult to interpret. Regardless, they created a picture, however incomplete, of the time in which Ralph lived, his activities, and relationships with friends and family. I found it particularly moving to read the postcards he sent home from France as a soldier during the First World War.

As my knowledge about Ralph's background and understanding of him grew, I began to see him more as a human being with hopes, dreams, and fears than just as a loved uncle and certainly more than a murder victim. I started this project because Ralph was murdered, and hence, I was focused on the law enforcement, medical, and legal aspects of the case. However, as time passed, I began to think of him more in terms of a person.

The impersonal dispassionate term "victim" easily conceals a person's humanity. Manfred Swartz expressed this fact in the

Not Just a Victim

book *Petra*, p.146, when reflecting on why he was going to write about the life of murdered Petra Kelly, the driving force behind the formation of the Green Party of Germany.[1]

> I'm not going to let you be the corpse at the top of the stairs. This is what I say to myself with some awareness that I'm being both grandiose and earnest. But still. There it is. You've been a corpse too long. I've let your final identity define you, your murder turn you into a murder victim, as though that's who you were, your meaning, your *self*.

I couldn't leave Ralph as a corpse at the side of the road.

Ralph at about 65.

A Pioneer Family

Ad Astra per Aspera
To the Stars with Difficulty
Kansas state motto adopted May 25, 1861

Ralph's parents, William and Sarah Snair, were among millions of Americans who were prompted to "go West" by the Homestead Act of 1862, coupled with the expansion of the railroad system. In the quarter century from the end of the Civil War in 1865 to 1890, the population of Kansas grew by more than one million people, making it the largest increase in the state's history. Today, the population is around three million.

In the spring of 1884, William and Sarah, and their two-year-old son, Charles, left their home in Ohio for the settlement now known as Zenda in southcentral Kansas. At the time, the town was named Rochester after Rochester, Minnesota, and later New Rochester. In 1892, it was renamed Zenda. According to legend, the unusual name was chosen because the wife of a Santa Fe Railroad conductor read the novel *The Prisoner of Zenda* and liked the name. Apparently, other townspeople did as well.

Pregnant during the trip west, Sarah gave birth months after their arrival to a daughter, also named Sarah. To avoid confusion the child was known by her middle name, Bertha. Two years later, Charles died at the age of four and was among the first to be buried in the Pleasant Hill Cemetery. Another son, Roland, was born in 1887, Ralph on February 28, 1890, and then three girls and a boy in the next ten years.

Ralph may have drawn his first breath in a sod house. Due to the scarcity of trees, many early settlers in the Zenda area, as elsewhere on the Great Plains, made use of sod to build their first homes. Some settlers also lived in dugouts. Regardless of the type of construction of the first Snair home, life was difficult but with much promise of better times in the future.

Many years later, in a letter to his son Don, Robert McCrory wrote of his grandparents' life in Zenda.

> The land was poor but they did get into cattle & did better. Those were such difficult days. He [William] had been thru a lot which may have made him a little hard nosed & tight with money.

About 1930, the Werner family bought the Snair homestead, which had a house and a barn on it. The barn was torn down, and the house moved. Most likely the house was a wood-frame structure, not the original structure constructed by the Snairs close to 50 years before.

Today, the land continues to be farmed by members of the Werner family. They alternate raising cattle with growing wheat, the common usages of land in the area since the 1880s. In spring 2018, Robin and I visited Donna Werner, the recent widow of Karl Werner. Karl is buried near little Charlie Snair in Pleasant Hill Cemetery in view of the Werner farm. Donna welcomed us into her home and shared her knowledge of her family and local history. She showed us the area around the former Snair property and the site of their home and barn.

Author at site of the house on the Snair homestead.

With a population of 79 and few operating businesses, Zenda today is much different than the town Ralph

A Pioneer Family

explored as a boy. When he was ten years old, in 1900, the bustling town had a population of approximately 1,400. For Zenda's centennial, Bonnie Bailey, a local historian, recreated the town's Main Street in miniature. Among her 36 tiny recreations on display in the local museum are a bank, grocery store, and lunch counter, plus newspaper and medical offices, and a wagon shop.

The original Geo. W. Ultch Lumber Co. building has been converted into a restaurant, aptly named the Lumber Yard. Robin and I lunched there with my cousins and sister in summer 2017 and again by ourselves in spring 2018. The restaurant is a popular place for locals to eat and talk. The weather and machinery, soil and crops undoubtedly figure prominently in the conversations of the men in jeans and boots, who come straight from the fields for their noon meal.

As the 19th century was ending, Ralph and his family relied on strong ties within their immediate and extended families, and the close-knit church community to meet the challenges of those demanding days. Every hand was needed to tackle the innumerable tasks required for survival. As a young boy, Ralph helped his father and older brother, Roland, in the fields and tended cattle. He also helped to care for the horses; their harnesses and the equipment required regular maintenance and frequent repair.

Around age six, Ralph started school at the Pleasant Hill School. His older siblings, Bertha and Roland, attended the same school.

Days started with family devotions and ended with prayer. Sundays were devoted to the Reformed Presbyterian Church, the centre of the family's social life. Considerable information exists about this church in Zenda. Ralph's family was among several families of this denomination from Ohio, Indiana, and Illinois to arrive in Zenda in the mid 1880s.

In his account of the early days, local historian W.G. Goenner[1] wrote:

> The year 1883 also brought a lot of Covenantors or Presbyterians who built the first church near Pleasant Hill School.

The church was built in 1886 with sixteen charter members. William Snair was certainly among them. Following closure of the church in 1886 and its sale in 1890, William participated in the church at Sterling.

Robert McCrory wrote:

> I admired my Grandpa and Grandma Snair. They were such a devout couple. He was such a godly man. During the 20 years they lived in Kingman Co. [where Zenda is located] he made a number of trips by horseback to the Sterling church for communion, presbytery meetings, Synod & etc.

The 60-mile, one-way trip to Sterling required three days on horseback.

Youth and Early Adulthood

In 1904, William and Sarah moved their family to Sterling because it had a well-established Reformed Presbyterian Church and a college. Originally called Peace, Sterling was established in 1871 and renamed four years later in honour of Sterling Rosan, an early settler. For over a century, the town has maintained a stable population. In 1910, there were 2,133 inhabitants, and today, the count is close to 2,400.

The Snairs sold their land in Zenda and moved to Sterling by horse and wagon. My mother told me her grandparents had driven their herd of cattle on the journey. In Sterling, they purchased land, built a home, and prospered. All of this, however, took time. The first few years were particularly rigorous. The oldest daughter, Bertha, delayed starting college for a year to stay home and help her mother. Over the years, the Snair home generated a wealth of memories as recalled decades later by Ralph's niece Zania (Vicki) Kay née Snair.

Long Time Dead

> I remember the farm at Sterling, the porch with the swing and Aunt Edna and Aunt Grace swinging to the moon, the round porch light. I remember eating watermelon and homemade ice cream and prayers on our knees in the dining room.

From early days, Sterling has been home to a variety of churches. The Reformed Presbyterian congregation was organized in 1877 by several families, whose descendants remain in the community. Ralph and his family regularly attended services at the white wood-frame church and held their own daily devotions on their knees at home. The Reformed Presbyterian denomination has continued to be an important part of the lives of members of succeeding generations.

The first Reformed Presbyterian congregation in North America was organized in 1743. A substantial proportion of the population of the colonies, Reformed Presbyterians were influential in the initiation and success of the Revolutionary War. Less than a century later, they served in the Union Army during the Civil War and formed part of the Underground Railroad, helping run away slaves to escape. Ralph's ancestors, who first set foot in the New World in the 1600s and 1700s, participated in the Revolutionary War and later in the fight against slavery.

Postcards in the album Don organized indicate Ralph's close association with the church community. In January 1907, Zada Patton, who was affiliated with the church's mission program, sent Ralph a postcard from Latakia,

Youth and Early Adulthood

Syria. She commented on the "quaint old way of getting water" shown in the picture of a horse-drawn water wheel on the front of the card. She wished Ralph well for the coming year and signed the card, "Your former S.S. [Sunday School] teacher and friend." A year later, Ralph received a card from Zada sent from Jerusalem. Eight years later, he got a postcard from Greeley, Colorado, with the message "Greetings from your S.S. Teacher. I wonder how everybody is this morning?"

Other postcards give glimpses into Ralph's work and family life. Charles McCrory, who would later marry Ralph's sister, Jessie, sent him a card while in Colorado Springs in 1913. A few months later, Charles mailed another card from his home in northeastern Kansas, commenting on the weather and that he and his brother were hauling fodder. Ralph visited Colorado in May 1916 and mailed a card to his sister Grace in Sterling.

The differences between the trajectory of Ralph's life and that of his siblings' lives started to become apparent in the first decades in Sterling. Neither family lore nor other lines of evidence indicate that his occupation was other than farm work prior to 1917. In May 1910, his father sent a card from Lake Winona, Indiana, asking Ralph how he was getting along farming. A few weeks later, Sarah wrote to her husband, "All is well. Ralph will soon be through the corn the second time."

All six of Ralph's brothers and sisters also worked at farm and house chores. As time passed, his siblings left home, married, and established their own homes; Ralph's life took a different course. He did not marry or make a home for himself. He lived in rented rooms and occasionally in small apartments. As a young man and for some years in mid-life, Ralph worked as a farm hand. He was also employed in various other capacities, such as handyman, factory worker, and assistant custodian.

Ralph's father, William, as was common at the time, did not receive formal schooling beyond Grade 8. He became a successful farmer, a respected church leader, and a loved family man. He encouraged his children to complete high school and pursue further education. In fact, the presence of a college was a major reason for relocating his family to Sterling.

Five of the Snair children attended Cooper College, a Presbyterian institution later renamed Sterling College. Bertha, Roland and Fravel became teachers, Edna had a career in business, and Grace became a registered nurse. Jessie, who did not attend college, devoted her life to being a homemaker.

Ralph may have terminated his schooling at Grade 8 when the family moved from Zenda to Sterling. He would have been a 14-year-old at the time. There is no evidence that Ralph attended and graduated from Sterling High School. His name does not appear in any editions of the local newspaper as a member of the graduating class.

There could have been several reasons why Ralph did not continue his schooling past Grade 8. He may have been uninterested, lacked aptitude, or not seen the need to continue his education to pursue a life of farming. His parents may have expected that he would eventually take over the farm and did not encourage further education.

In postcards written by Ralph's father and other members of the family, a good command of the English language is demonstrated. Those written by Ralph have misspellings and poor grammar.

Changes

RALPH W SNAIR
Kansas
P VT MED DET56 INFANTRY
WORLD WAR I PH
FEB 28 1890 APRIL 19 1957
Inscription on gravestone,
Sterling Cemetery

Ralph's life centred around the farm, family, and church until June 5, 1917, when he enlisted in the United States Army for service in the First World War. He was 27 years old. In the following 22 months, Ralph's worldview would expand exponentially. He encountered men from many dissimilar backgrounds and with religious beliefs and moral values different from his. He was exposed to another language and culture in a country far from home. He saw firsthand the horror of battlefield causalities and death, and eventually, he would join the ranks of the injured.

Long Time Dead

Ralph in US Army uniform.

On June 5, Sterling townspeople gathered to give the young men who had enlisted that day a sober and heartfelt send off. The *Sterling Bulletin* reported on the events.

> Registration Day was fittingly observed in this city Tuesday when one hundred eight of the young men of the city and Sterling township enrolled themselves for the defence of their country. Everywhere there was a spirit of earnestness manifested and the serious features of the occasion

Changes

> overshadowed all other thoughts and forbade anything in the way of a holiday celebration of the day. There was a complete absence of any effort on the part of the young men in this community to evade the registration and those eligible began presenting themselves early in the morning.

In the evening, city officials led a parade of the young men, who carried a banner with the motto "We Will Be Brave." The parade ended at the opera house, where a short patriotic program was held. Mrs. J. W. Dill was among the speakers. As a mother of three sons and a son-in-law, who had registered that day, she addressed the anxiety of all mothers "for the physical and moral welfare of the boys."

Some of the "boys" never came home, their bodies in graves overseas or lost in foreign soil. The bodies of others were returned for burial in their home country. Among those who returned alive were men with life-altering physical, psychological, and emotional injuries. Ralph, along with many others, suffered from poisonous gases used for the first time as weapons during wartime. A Purple Heart medal was awarded to Ralph in recognition of his injuries as indicated by the letters PH on his gravestone.

Two months before that sombre June day in Sterling, the United States had declared war on Germany, joining the fight that had begun in summer 1914 when the Allies—France, Great Britain, Belgium, Russia, and Serbia—lined up against Germany and the Austro-Hungarian Empire.

Long Time Dead

On May 8, 1917, Congress passed the Selective Service Act, which resulted in the draft of 2.8 million men.

When Ralph enlisted, he gave his trade as farming and that he was employed on a farm near Sterling. He described himself as medium height, black hair, not bald with brown eyes, and no disabilities. His father was listed as next-of-kin. When he returned to the United States from France in March, 1919, his medical condition was given as "walking wounded with no dressing."

An affable man, Ralph undoubtedly bonded closely with fellow soldiers during his time in the army. He kept in contact with some comrades after the war. In December 1919, following his return home, he received a postcard from a former fellow soldier residing in Lee, Massachusetts.

> Wishing you a Merry Xmas & Prosperous Year. Sincerely M.T. Deeling. I often think of those seasons in Texas. If we only had some of that heat here. Everything is fine.

What is known about Ralph's time during the war comes from postcards and letters written by him, articles in the hometown newspaper, a brief biographical sketch in the book *History of the Descendants of John Hottel*[1] and his final payment stub from the army. The payment stub is the only piece of Ralph's file to survive the fire on July 22, 1973, at the National Personnel Records Center in St. Louis, Missouri, which destroyed the major portion of all records of army personnel from 1912 through 1959.

Changes

The earliest information about Ralph's wartime experiences are two postcards that were written over a year after he enlisted. He wrote the cards while stationed at Camp MacArthur in Waco, Texas. Camp MacArthur was a military training camp set up ten weeks after the United States declared war on Germany. It covered over 10,000 acres of farmland and consisted of administration offices, a tent city, and various military buildings. There was a hospital which nurse Loretta Johnston described in 1918 as a "pleasant place for sick and convalescent soldiers."[2] The hospital had a recreation hall where parties and dances for nurses and officers were held. Camp MacArthur was officially closed on March 7, 1919, and the land became part of the city of Waco.

Camp MacArthur.

Long Time Dead

The first card Ralph sent from Waco was postmarked June 16, 1918, and addressed to his sister, Grace, in Sterling. As he frequently did, he wrote in pencil. On the front is a photograph of two soldiers with several one-story buildings and tents in the background.

> How are all the folks. We are still in quarantine. We expected to get out the 12th and when that came they told us ___ [undecipherable word] and they say four more days yet so that will make it next Tuesday. How far is harvest off yet? I don't know whether I will get home or not. If I was in my regular company I could find out but can't find out anything not even get your mail I have not had any mail a week ago today. We are getting pretty mad about it. It has been a 100 degrees down here that seems pretty hot when the wind is not blowing. June 14. Ralph.

The second card was postmarked June 20 and mailed to his father. A photograph of a one-story wooden building on pylons, which served as the YMCA Headquarters, is on the front of the card.

> I am feeling pretty good. The Rice Co. bunch of boys were split up today. I was moved to my new place this morning. My address is 7 Division, Medical Supply

Changes

Depot, Camp MacArthur, Waco, Texas.
Write soon. June 18.

In the first card, Ralph mentioned having been quarantined. Four days later, presumably written when he was out of quarantine, he wrote that he was "feeling pretty good." This phrase rather than simply saying he was good may imply that he had been ill. He was at Camp MacArthur during the early phase of the 1918–1919 influenza epidemic. It is not clear whether he was quarantined because he was ill or because the quarantine was part of a widespread effort to prevent soldiers from acquiring the influenza virus.

Strict wartime censorship of the severity and spread of the disease was in effect and was aimed at keeping up public morale. The appearance of the flu in the spring of 1918 in US military camps and some cities was the first wave of the pandemic. Most deaths occurred during the brutal second wave, primarily in the 16-week period between mid-September to mid-December 1918. The third and final phase, which was serious but not as lethal, began in early 1919 and ran through spring. The disease continued to circulate seasonally worldwide for the next 38 years.

Studies identify the first known outbreak of epidemic influenza, commonly and incorrectly called Spanish Influenza, as occurring at Camp Funston, a temporary training camp located at Fort Riley in Kansas. Considerable epidemiological evidence suggests that epidemic influenza had occurred earlier about 160 miles southwest of Sterling in Haskell County, Kansas. In this sparsely inhabited area, people grew grain and lived in close proximity to poultry, cattle, and hogs. Sod houses were common. A local physician in the area, Dr. Loring Milner, recognized in the first weeks of 1918 that he was dealing with an unusual influenza-like disease and warned national public health officials.

Camp Funston, the second largest of 16 temporary training camps in the country, was critical in the spread of the influenza-like disease. Young farmers from Haskell County reported to the camp for training, as did thousands of men from all parts of the Midwest. Funston was more like a city than a camp and, on average, held more than 50,000 young soldiers. In addition to housing and training facilities, the camp had general stores, theatres, and social centres. Family and friends picked up the virus when they visited the camp. Soldiers, on leave and not yet showing signs of the disease, took the virus into the greater community. The soldiers also moved to other army bases, such as Camp MacArthur, where Ralph was stationed, and were eventually sent to France, taking the virus with them.

Somewhere between 50 and 100 million people globally are estimated to have died in the influenza pandemic. Regardless of the number, the flu caused the deaths of many times more people than the nine million soldiers estimated to have been killed in combat during the First World War. The enormous impact of the disease is directly related to the mass movement of troops and their close living quarters in the trenches and encampments.

France

On a cold, grey, drizzly day one hundred years after the signing of the Armistice on November 11, 1918, I joined hundreds of others in a city park to remember and honour those Allied soldiers who served and died in the First World War. I thought of Ralph and of what he had experienced—the filth, the blood, the shock of being gassed, and the long convalescence. Ralph was among the lucky ones who came home, many forever changed.
Susan McIver 2018

On August 4, 1918, Ralph left the United States and, days later, landed on European soil at Brest, France, on the western edge of the continent. Brest was a major disembarkation point for the American Expeditionary Forces. Upon arrival in France, Ralph went into training for first aid work and served in the medical detachment of the 56th Infantry Regiment in the US 6th Infantry Division.

The 56th Infantry's primary service in France was during the Meuse–Argonne Offensive. More specifically the 56th was located on the left bank of the Moselle River and was the American military unit nearest to the German city of Metz, now part of France. Preparations were being made to attack Metz when the Armistice was signed.

The Meuse–Argonne Offensive, which started September 26, 1918, and ended 47 days later November 11, 1918, was one of a series of Allied attacks known overall as the Hundred Days Offensive. The Meuse–Argonne Offensive involved both American and French troops and was bordered on one end by the Meuse River and the thick, rugged terrain of the Argonne Forest on the other. One of the largest, if not the largest, military engagements in American history, the offensive involved 1.2 million US soldiers and was among the deadliest, resulting in 26,277 deaths. American losses were exacerbated by the inexperience of many of the troops, the tactics used during the early phases of the operation, and the wide-spread onset of influenza.

Four postcards in the album give glimpses into the time between Ralph's arrival and the final stages of the war. He wrote the cards while stationed in Bragelogne, a town in the Grand Est region of the country. At various times, the region has been called the Champagne-Ardennes region or the Alsace-Champagne-Ardenne-Lorraine region. This region is less than 100 miles east of Paris and is made up of the four departments: Aube, Marne, Haute-Marne, and Ardennes. Portions of these departments saw fierce and bloody fighting by US troops in the final two and a half months of the war.

The faded, grey postcards appear to be part of a series of least six cards, although numbers three and four are missing.

France

Sent by military mail, the cards do not bear postmarks. From information on the cards, we can deduce that he sent the cards after having been at the front or while he was at the front. Here are the messages Ralph wrote on the cards and a description of the photographs on the front of them:

> *No. 1*: This is a bird's eye view of the city where we stayed for a month and a half or two months and drilled before we went to the front. It has 360 people in it. It's more a country town than a city. I think the people thought the world of us. It is the first time any American soldiers were ever placed in it and I guess is why they thought so much of us.
>
> *(Photo on front: General countryside view. Written on front: Bragelogne (Aube), 360 hab.)*
>
> *No. 2*: This is the main avenue or grand avenue or whatever you want to call it. The building to the right, the one fairly cut off, is the hotel of the city. It is called the White Horse Hotel as you can see a white horse out in front over the gate. Notice--that boy has an apron on--that is their way all of the little boys are dressed so to keep their clothes clean. They never wear overalls.

Long Time Dead

(Photo on front: Main Street of Bragelogne showing buildings and four people: two adult men, two children--a boy and a girl. White horse sign is visible. Written on front: Bragelogne (Aube) Grande Rue.)

Bragelogne, France.

No. 5: This is the picture of the house of richest man that lives in this town. He doesn't live there just his wife and two little boys. He was with the French Army he [*sic*] is an adjutant with the army. His two little boys would come over to our infirmary almost everyday and we would have a big time.

France

(Photo on front: Large house with a small boy with a watering can and walking stick on path to the house. Written on front: Bragelogne (Aube) "Ancien Chateau.)

The infirmary Ralph mentioned would have been where he worked as a member of the medical detachment.

No. 6: This is the church it is about two hundred years old and it looks it from the inside moss was growing on the walls. I went there every Sabbath day I could go to church but I would not understand it because was all in French. I got tired of carrying these cards around with me and they are getting worn so I thought I would send them to you Grace as of [*sic*] you could keep them till I get home. Your brother Ralph.

(Photo on front: country church. Written on front: Bragelogne (Abe) L'Eglise. Collection J. Chapron.)

Gassed

Staggering, dumbfounded and stupefied, they were brought in, after having been conveyed from the ambulance to the train. However, once too much gas had been inhaled its action has the same effect upon the lungs as a slow process of drowning.
J. Clinton Morrison, p.78, in *Rush to Danger: Medics in the Line of Fire*. 2019. Ted Barris. Harper Collins. Toronto. 406 pp.

On November 1, only ten days before the Armistice was signed, Ralph was gassed near Metz. As recorded in his final payment statement, he suffered from "deleterious absorption of inhaled mustard gas." He was one of the 19,000 American troops who were gassed in the Meuse–Argonne Offensive.

Chemical warfare in the form of gas was a hallmark of the First World War. Gas caused relatively few deaths, but the psychological impact was great. It was one of the most feared weapons of the war. Application was imprecise, and

Gassed

air currents could carry clouds of gas away from targets and onto unintended troops or nearby villages.

Both sides of the conflict used several types of gasses, such as chlorine, phosgene, and mustard, individually or in combination. Phosgene is estimated to have been responsible for 85 percent of the 91,000 gas deaths in the war. Its high toxicity is due to it reacting with proteins in the alveoli of the lungs, which causes a build up of fluids and leads to suffocation. Phosgene is more deadly than chlorine, which reacts with water in the lungs to form hydrochloric acid. Chlorine can also damage the eyes to the point of blindness.

Mustard gas, the most widely used gas in the First World War, is an irritant and vesicant causing chemical burns on contact, the resulting blisters oozing yellow liquid. If inhaled, the gas can damage lung tissue, which swells and may result in death. Although it had a low mortality rate of two to three percent of gas deaths, it was responsible for thousands of causalities and much suffering both during the war and after soldiers returned home.

Combat soldiers and those who served in the medical detachment were particularly vulnerable to gas attacks. The non-medical professionals in the detachment, such as Ralph, did exceedingly dangerous jobs. At the front line, they performed first aid and placed the wounded on stretchers, which they carried, often over long distances, to ambulances.

Ralph wrote a letter to his family from Mantes, France, on February 15, 1919, while on his way home and still recovering from gas-related injuries. The letter was published in the *Sterling Bulletin* in the section "Letters from Soldier Boys" on March 13, 1919.

> Mantes, France, Feb. 15, 1919. Dear Folks at Home: Will try and write a few more lines this week, to let you know I have made a stey [step] toward home. About three hundred of us left Base Hospital 210 on a Red Cross Train for Mantes. Its in the southern part of France, close to the seaport St. Mazair [Nazair]. We are in evacuating hospital 28. They say we won't be here long, that we will be sent to another hospital, quarantined for four days, examined, deloused and get a bath, new clothes and get on the boat, but you can't believe every thing you hear. It is pretty warm here besides what it is at Toul. There snow was on the ground here the ground is not frozen in the evening. I am feeling pretty fair. Will close for this time. Will not give you my address as I won't be here long. Your son, Ralph Snair.

The Saint Mihiel and Meuse–Argonne offensives were launched from the Toul area in northeastern France. A group of hospitals at Toul was originally formed in part to meet the needs imposed by the Saint Mihiel operation. Later, the Justice Hospital Group was organized at the same location. Toul was the location of Base Hospital 210 Ralph mentioned in his letter.

There was a large inflow and outflow of patients at the hospital in Toul because of its proximity to major operations. For weeks, over 1,000 soldiers were admitted every day, and on one day, 1,544 wounded and gassed patients were received. Most admissions were stretcher cases, who had to be transported recumbent up as many as four stories by stretcher bearers. All supplies—clothing, bedding, and surgical material—had to be carried up and down. The patients' bodily wastes and garbage had to be taken down the stairs by hand.

A Bessonneau tent, a large timber and canvas portable structure, served as a receiving ward and sorting station for the gas hospital. A corner was screened-off for treatment of phosgene patients, who were immediately administered oxygen and treated. Mustard gas cases were sent to a building equipped with two French portable bathing machines supplied with running water. The marked shock of phosgene gas cases and the sloughing of the respiratory mucosa of mustard gas cases were the most striking clinical phenomena noted. Some of the buildings were used for mild cases of mustard gassing and for convalescents recovering from exposure to phosgene gas.

March 4, 1919, Ralph left Brest, on board the ship *America*, originally a German vessel launched in 1905 as SS *Amerika*. A passenger liner, she sailed primarily between Hamburg and New York. At the onset of the First World War, she was docked in Boston, where she remained for three years to avoid seizure by the British Royal Navy. Hours before entry of the United States into the war, *Amerika* was seized and later transferred to the US Navy for use as a troop transport ship. Her name anglicized to *America*, she transported almost 40,000 troops to France, and after the Armistice, brought over 51,000 troops home.

Carrying war weary, homesick troops, Ralph among them, the *America* arrived in the United States on March 13, 1919, at Hoboken, New Jersey, a primary US Army Port of Embarkation during the First World War. Approximately three million soldiers passed through the city. The slogan "Heaven, Hell or Hoboken by Christmas" was used by General John J. Pershing, leader of the American Expeditionary Forces, to rally troops with hope of an early return home.

Upon arrival at Hoboken, March 13, 1919, Ralph was sent directly to Hospital #3 in New York, NY. Eight days later, he was transferred to the Detachment Convalescent Centers at Camp Funston, Fort Riley, Kansas. On April 7, Ralph was paid $6,637.12 and discharged. With 22 months of military service, including five months in hospital behind him, he boarded the train for home.

Coming Home and Seeking Help

Ralph returned home to a nation weary of war, recovering from the influenza pandemic, and eager for change. Between 1920 and 1929, the Roaring Twenties, the nation's total wealth more than doubled. For the first time, more Americans lived in cities than on farms. The decade was marked by a feeling of novelty, modernity, and breaking with traditions. Automobiles, electric appliances, motion pictures, jazz, and flappers had arrived on the scene, and there was a sense that everything was possible through technology. These attitudes were especially prevalent in the big cities. People in rural areas, such as those in Kansas, continued in their more conservative lifestyles and were uncomfortable with some of the changes.

Although the 1920s were a time of general prosperity for the country, not all farming communities, including some in Kansas, benefitted. For many farmers, the times were so challenging that agricultural organizations implored Congress to pass relief legislation to forestall bankruptcy. Subsidies designed to provide relief for farmers became an issue of major contention. Between 1924 and 1928, various bills to counteract falling agricultural prices were either defeated in Congress or vetoed by President Calvin Coolidge. The son of a Vermont famer, Coolidge thought that relief measures would not help farmers, but rather would benefit exporters, while expanding federal bureaucracy. Instead of the federal government becoming involved in manipulating prices, Coolidge preferred to increase profitability by modernizing agriculture. A conservative, he encouraged business, such as the budding aviation industry. Ralph would be briefly employed in that industry in the early 1940s.

Soon after returning home, Ralph had apparently recovered sufficiently from his gas injuries to seek work. On June 1, 1919, Cecil Hays sent a postcard from Superior, Nebraska to Ralph in Sterling.

> Well Ralph I sort of run off & left you didn't I. Well if you come I can get you all kinds of work good wages too. Write and tell what your [*sic*] going to do.

Later in 1919, Ralph sent a card from Hutchinson to his brother Fravel in Sterling.

> How are all of you today. I am feeling fine. I have been working for the I.S.C. of America for a while but they got thru with me this morning so if I don't scare up a job

Coming Home and Seeking Help

> by tonight I am going to Wichita. Heard
> there is lots work.

The reason Ralph did not resume fulltime work on the family farm in the months following his return home is unknown. His father was a prosperous farmer, so paying Ralph should not have been difficult. Perhaps Ralph wanted to chart his own course in life in larger cities or he never regained the robust health needed for the physical demands of farm work.

According to postcards, Ralph sought help for health problems on at least three occasions from early 1921 through early 1924. For over a month in early 1921, Ralph was at the Invalids' Hotel and Surgical Institute, part of the World's Dispensary Medical Association, in Buffalo, New York. A card postmarked 1922 indicates that he was able to work following his release from the Buffalo facility. Three years after Buffalo, he was in Lampasas, Texas, home of purported curative mineral springs, and shortly thereafter at the Battle Creek Sanitarium in Battle Creek, Michigan.

On the trip to Buffalo, Ralph sent a postdated dated February 10, 1921, to Grace. A photograph of Lasalle Street Station in Chicago is on the front.

> Hello Grace. I got here at 9:15 this morning. Will leave for Buffalo at 5:00 this afternoon and get there at 7:00 in the morning. It is cloudy and foggy here getting colder. I am feeling good. Ralph.

Long Time Dead

The following day, February 11, he wrote a postcard to his father.

> Well, I got here at seven o'clock this morning and went right to the hospital. I was examined and will have to take a moth's [*sic*] treatment here will right [*sic*] and tell you more about each thing here.

Over the following weeks, Ralph received numerous postcards addressed to the World's Dispensary Medical Association in Buffalo. Many of those cards were on occasion of his 31st birthday. His mother sent him a card postmarked February 25, with a painting of a bridge over a stream and farm buildings bordered by large irises. On the reverse side she wrote:

> Dear Ralph. I suppose you know today is your birthday. Hope you are getting better and soon will be home feeling alright. Papa is getting some ground ready for oats. Mother.

The album contains two postcards Ralph sent to Grace with comments about his health. On February 21, he wrote that he was feeling "pretty good" even though he had a bad cold. Over three weeks later, he wrote a postcard which included:

Coming Home and Seeking Help

> Dear Grace and all the Rest. How are all you folks this afternoon. I am getting better a little all the time. The doctor told me yesterday that I have to stay ten days longer so will be out the 23rd. I saw the Falls Thursday. They were great.

Whatever Ralph's specific health problems were and the reason for his extended stay, he was able to visit Niagara Falls while still a patient.

Following release from the Buffalo facility, Ralph sent a card to Grace while visiting relatives in Ohio. It was postmarked March 25, Mount Vernon. His message included, "I am feeling fine here in Ohio."

Over a year later, March 28, 1922, Ralph mailed a postcard from Wichita with a photograph on the front of the new Wichita city library to Grace in Sterling.

> Fri. How are all the folks? How is Bertha getting along? I am feeling good so far. I am working in a impliment [sic] store. They handle the Oliver line. I help set up machinery and do other odd jobs. Has it been raining at Sterling it [sic] sure has here. They say the river is up. I have never been over to see it. There are sure lots of cripples here to get healed. R.S.

From this card, we know that in the spring of 1922, Ralph was working in Wichita and had questionable health, hence the phrase "feeling good so far." It is unknown if his reference on the card to cripples and their search for healing had any connection to his own health.

Almost two years later, on January 1, 1924, Ralph sent a card to Grace from Lampasas, Texas, the home of mineral springs known for centuries for their health-giving properties. On the front of the card is a photograph labelled "playground of Lampasas," showing small cabins in a park-like setting.

> Hello: Grace. How are you this morning. I am feeling fine. I got [here] yesterday evening about 6 o'clock. This is not a very big place about 3,000 people. The country___ [undecipherable word] here. Love, Ralph.

A month later, February 1, 1924, Ralph was in at the Sanitarium in Battle Creek, Michigan. He must have purchased the card in Lampasas because on the front is a photograph labelled "Cottages in Anderson Park. Lampasas, Texas." Anderson Park was taken over by the Baptist Church and became part of Hancock Park, the site of a large bathing resort.

> Hello Grace. How are you folks this afternoon? I am feeling fine. The sun is shining bright today the [*sic*] first time it has shown real bright since I have been here. I am on a milk diet now. I think I will change Drs

Coming Home and Seeking Help

> today. I don't like my Dr. How is B. Mc
> and the kids. I suppose Will has got back
> from home by this time. Ralph.

On February 5, Ralph again sent a card from Battle Creek to Grace. On the front is a photograph of a large industrial plant with the caption "The largest manufacturers of ready to eat cereal foods in the world."

> I am in this place right now writing this
> [*sic*] it is a nice clean place and it sure is a
> big place. The food that goes out is perfect
> [*sic*] clean as I was all thru it. Ralph.

Kellogg cereal production plant.

Long Time Dead

This is the last postcard from Ralph in the album until 1943.

Available records do not give the specific health problems underlying Ralph's visits to Buffalo, Lampasas, and Battle Creek. It is known from his postcards that on admission to the Invalids' Hotel and Surgical Institute in Buffalo on February 11, 1921, he was told that he would need a month-long treatment. Several weeks later, the doctor had told him he would have to extend his treatment by ten days. At the time, he reported getting gradually better.

On a card with birthday wishes postmarked February 28, 1921, Ralph's brother Roland, who was living in Kiowa, Kansas at the time wrote:

> How are you Ralph! It was quite a surprise to us when we read in the Bulletin that you were in Buffalo. Hope you get along OK. You ought to have lots of time to write us a letter and tell us everything and why you went to Buffalo to take treatments.

Apparently, Ralph did not share the reason(s) for seeking help with all members of his family. In fact, he may have been reticent to speak about his health problems in detail with anyone. The only clue about his condition is contained in the card he sent from the Battle Creek Sanitarium three years later in which he mentioned being on a milk diet.

Whatever the specific reasons, they were likely related to his injury from being gassed during service in the First World War. In addition to well-recognized physical damage, it is not unreasonable to think that Ralph may have had long-lasting

Coming Home and Seeking Help

psychological and emotional difficulties. His milk diet at the Battle Creek Sanitarium is indicative of gastrointestinal problems, most likely ulcers. No mention is made on Ralph's final pay stub of what was then termed shell shock, now likely diagnosed as post-traumatic stress disorder (see "Appendix 1: Psychological Impact of Military Conflict"). Perhaps he was among the thousands of men whose lives were compromised by symptoms of shell shock, which appeared after the war and could involve physical as well as psychological difficulties.

Service in the medical corps would have exposed Ralph to horrific scenes of injury and death. With his first aid training, he may have served as a stretcher bearer, removing injured soldiers from the front lines and being exposed to the intense sounds of artillery and gunfire. It might have been in this capacity that he was gassed. Perhaps his work was in the crowded, chaotic first aid stations and field hospitals. Once gassed, he became a patient himself, undergoing initial treatment near the front and later spending four months in hospital before returning home.

Prior to 1917, when Ralph enlisted in the army at age 27, his life appeared to be stable, centred on family, farm, and church. After his return home in 1919, his life seemed to be less focused. He never settled on a particular type of work and never married or created a home for himself, always living in rented rooms or small apartments when not with his parents. A shortage of money may have been the reason Ralph did not own a car and may have been why his sisters and brother-in-law were to buy him clothes. In fact, a shortage of funds may have been a factor in his becoming associated with the person(s) who eventually shot him.

Dark Days

October 29, 1929, the New York Stock Market crashed with dramatic economic, social, and political results. Although there had been indications earlier in the year of a distressed economy, historians consider the October '29 crash as the beginning of the severe, prolonged economic downtown now known as the Great Depression. The timing and severity of the depression varied in different countries, but the eventual impact of the crash, which started in the United States, was global.

The suffering of the people of Kansas, including Ralph and his family, and those in neighbouring states was compounded by the drought that led to the Dust Bowl, a series of dust storms that began in 1930 and lasted until 1941. The Dust Bowl had its origin in the increased demand for wheat during the First World War, which caused many thousands of acres covered by the native prairie grass to be tilled. In the 1920s, wheat prices fell and those acres became fallow. At the same time, new mechanized farm machinery came on the market. These machines made cultivating crops, customarily done in straight rows, much easier.

Dark Days

Topsoil was easily picked up by the ever-present prairie winds and formed the huge clouds of dust that characterized the Depression in the Midwest.

> On Sunday, April 14, 1935, called Black Sunday, a massive front moved across the Great Plains from the northwest. Packing winds of 60 miles per hour, the loose topsoil was scooped up and mounded into billowing clouds of dust hundreds of feet high. People hurried home, for to be caught outside could mean suffocation and death. The dust and darkness halted all forms of transportation, and the fine silt sifting through any draft or joint forced the close of hospitals, flour mills, schools, and businesses.[1]

Plunging wheat prices caused many banks to close. The total farm value of the agricultural production of Kansas in the 1930s was 63 percent of what it was during the 1920s. The 1930s was the only decade in which Kansas lost population.[2] Some people, especially in the worst areas in Western Kansas and Oklahoma, left their homes and headed west. In 1939, the Nobel Prize winning author John Steinbeck wrote what is considered his best work, *The Grapes of Wrath*,[3] which tells the story of Oklahoma farmers, who left their dust-shrouded homes to go to California and become migrant workers.

Long Time Dead

Other Dust Bowl residents stayed, fortified by hope, faith, and stubbornness. A large number of unemployed men moved from the cities to return to their family farm. Ralph was among them. The federal census of 1930 has Ralph residing on North Broadway in Sterling with his parents and Grace. Although the Snairs were living in town, their farm continued to be worked, almost certainly by Ralph, perhaps with the help of hired hands, and to some extent by his aging father.

During the worst years of the Great Depression, Ralph endured times of personal sadness following the deaths of family members. In 1933, his sister Bertha, my grandmother, died following a long period of declining health, which started with an automobile accident in the 1920s. She left a husband and three young children, including my mother, who remembered that the family did not have the money needed to seek health care for her mother.

I have a haunting photograph of my sombre, dejected-looking grandparents and their three children taken around 1930. In the picture, my grandmother appears nothing like the vibrant young woman in the photograph taken when she rode a mule to the bottom of the Grand Canyon, dressed in a split skirt and wearing a bonnet, in 1909 or in the picture of her and my handsome grandfather on their wedding day in 1912.

To compound the family's misfortune, in 1933, the same year his wife died, my grandfather lost the family farm due to poor crops during the desperate conditions of the Depression. Edna, Grace, and Ralph stepped in to help fill the void left by my grandmother. A year later, Ralph's

Dark Days

mother, my great grandmother, Sarah Cathryn died of natural causes at age 78.

The Second World War helped to end the Depression by creating a demand for food and an increase in the price of Kansas products. Farmers, however, were faced with price ceilings for their wheat, production quotas, and shortages of farm machinery along with the movement of hired hands to well-paid factory jobs. During the war, Wichita became a major manufacturing centre for the aircraft industry, attracting tens of thousands of underemployed workers from farms and small towns. In the early 1940s, Ralph was employed by the Boeing Company in Wichita. During the war, farmers lobbied Congress to ensure that young farmers were deferred from the draft. This meant my father, unlike Ralph during the First World War, raised wheat in Kansas rather than carry a rifle overseas.

Ralph's father, William Allan, died from natural causes in 1941 at age 84. In his will, William bequeathed one-half of a quarter section of land to Ralph and Grace. On October 8, 1942, they sold the property to Calvin L. Young for $6,250. They would have each received $3,125 minus any legal or realtor fees. The other four living Snair siblings and Bertha's three children received the proceeds from the sale of three parcels of lands and William's personal effects. The proceeds were divided equally into five shares.

After his father's death, Ralph moved to Wichita, the largest city in the state. It grew rapidly from close to 115,000 residents in 1940 to 168,000 in 1950, and by 1960 to 255,000. Today, the population is approximately 395,000.

Long Time Dead

On July 26, 1943, Ralph sent a postcard to Edna and her husband in Hutchinson. A photograph of the Wichita Municipal Airport is on the front.

> Hello Edna and Charley: How are you folks this morning? I am O.K. Has it been hot over there? It is a fright here. Got a card from Grace Sat. telling about Mrs. Boyle's death. That sure is to [*sic*] bad. I wonder what he will do? That Friday night I was at your placed it rained about four inches here in Wichita. I am doing some repair work and painting on the folks' garage where I room. They [word missing] me because painters are hard to get. I have picked up 4 lbs since I quit Boeings. Ralph.

Implied in Ralph's message is that working in the aircraft industry had been difficult for whatever reason and had resulted in unwanted weight loss. Perhaps the difficulty was due to the possibility that he had never returned to robust health after the war. He was able to do physical work, such as small painting jobs and even farm labour, but these may have been less demanding than his factory tasks.

Not quite three months later October 15, 1943, he sent another postcard to Edna and Charles with news of misfortune. A picture of St. Francis Hospital in Wichita is on the front of the card.

Dark Days

> Yesterday the 13th was unlucky for me. As I was going to breakfast a woman ran her car into me knocked me down. Busted the small bone in my leg sprained the other ankle and cut a gash in the side of head which took 3 stiches to close. It will be six weeks before I can walk on that broken leg. I wonder if you and Grace can come and get my clothes out of that [*sic*] so that woman can rent the room to someone else. Ralph.

Ralph's residence in Wichita was interrupted by at least two years starting in 1945 when he worked on farms near Enid, Oklahoma. According to the 1952 Wichita city directory, Ralph was living on Main Street. His occupation was given as assistant custodian. Two years later, his occupation was the same and his place of residence had changed to 142 N. Chautauqua Avenue. In the 1956 directory, he had the same address. No occupation was listed because he had retired by that time.

How did Ralph occupy his time when not working? There is scant mention of anything relevant in police records. Although reported as religious, he apparently was not an active participant in a church. He did not have a car, a hobby, or a garden and did not hunt or fish, or engage in other outdoor sports. Television was nonexistent for most of his life and only in its infancy in his latter years. From all indications, he was not an avid reader or letter writer. The daily newspaper and radio may have been his only diversions at home. He may have met a friend or acquaintance for coffee or dropped by a pool hall for a game.

The last time I saw Ralph was in the summer of 1955, when my parents, sister, and I visited him at his Chautauqua residence. I remember his gentle demeanour and warm smile. It was easy to see why my mother was so fond of him.

PART IV

Suspects

Warren Arthur Girvin

Within hours of the discovery of Ralph's body investigators met their first murder suspect—Warren Arthur Girvin. Age 32, Warren was visiting his parents, Garrett and Edna Mae Girvin, at their Wichita home when investigators arrived in the early hours of Saturday, April 20, to interview them. Employed as a truck driver, Warren resided with his wife and stepdaughter in Raytown, Missouri, a suburb of Kansas City, Missouri. The length of his visit in Wichita—overnight or longer—is unknown.

Investigators' interest in Warren would be prompted because he knew Ralph from previous visits to his parents' home and his extensive criminal history and psychiatric problems. Agent Lansdowne wrote that Warren "had been arrested numerous times for just about everything in the books" and "also had been a mental patient."

Special Agent Howard L. Docker found that Warren had been employed by Jack Cooper Transport Co., headquartered in Kansas City, Missouri, for the past six years. He did not have a record with the Kansas City police department; however, he did have a file with the FBI, number 1837476.

Warren Arthur Girvin

Regarding Warren's physical and mental health, Agent Docker wrote in his report of May 2, 1957, that Warren was currently in a medical clinic in Snyder, Texas, with a purported sprained back. In the past, he had been a patient at the public psychiatric facility in the city of Nevada in Missouri.

At the time of Ralph's murder, Warren drove a light-blue and cream coloured 1956 Pontiac sedan. Unable to determine the exact make of tires of Warren's truck, Agent Docker believed them to be either Firestone or US Royal. Recording such information may have been a routine matter or suspicious tire tracks had been noticed at the scene. This is the only instance in the KBI file that hinted a car other than the rented car had been at the scene.

Based on information in the driver's log, Ray Hobson, the supervisor of the transport company, provided a history of Warren's whereabouts, starting on March 28, 1957. Of interest was that Warren arrived in Emporia at 1:30 a.m. on April 17 and remained there for 12.5 hours. At 2:00 p.m., he left for Kansas City, arriving at 5:59 p.m. He was off work until April 22, 1957. Ralph was murdered in the pre-dawn hours of April 19. Warren's whereabouts during the critical hours of the night of August 18–19 is unknown. Investigators met him at his parents' home in Wichita in the early hours of April 20. There is no mention of his arrival time.

Subsequent investigation by Agent Kline found that Warren had not registered on April 17 at any of the Jack Cooper Transport Company's authorized motels and hotels in Emporia. Mr. Hobson said it was not unusual for Warren to sleep in his truck. Why Agent Kline was interested in Warren's whereabouts in Emporia from 1:30 a.m. until 2:00 p.m. on April 17 is not evident. Any contact with Ralph seems to have been impossible on the 17th because Ralph rented the Ford in Wichita at 3:00 p.m., an hour after Warren had left for Kansas City, and had driven only about 75 miles by the time he purchased five gallons of gasoline early Thursday morning, April 18. It is possible, however, that Warren and Ralph could have met in Emporia or elsewhere on the 18th.

Warren was an unsavoury and potentially violent man. Mr. Hobson said he was so unpopular with the other drivers that if he broke down in the road, they would pass by without picking him up or helping in any way.

Assistant chief of police for Raytown, Missouri, Marion Beeler, told Agents Kline and Lansdowne on May 9 that he had "handled" Warren Girvin in May or June of 1956. Warren's wife, Clara Nadine, had laid a complaint that he had attempted to have intercourse with her ten-year-old daughter from a previous relationship. Clara Nadine was Warren's third wife. They had met in Emporia, and at the time of their marriage in 1953, she was a waitress at Fred's Derby Truck Stop.

When picked up by Assistant Chief Beeler, Warren readily admitted he had criminal tendencies and spoke of his record, starting as a juvenile. He said he had a violent temper and had knocked a hole in one of the doors at home with his fist and torn up some furniture. He also said the one thing he feared most was his wife divorcing him.

Warren did not have a gun at the time according to the KBI file.

To get help for him, the assistant chief referred Warren to a physician in Raytown, who in turn referred him to the psychiatric section of the Kansas University Medical Center.

The Raytown physician said he had seen Mr. Girvin several times, and in his opinion, Warren was a psychopath and paranoid, who could be very dangerous if sufficiently aroused. Although Warren stated he was sorry for his actions and asked for forgiveness, the physician was not convinced he was sincere. The physician thought Warren was "the type of person who would do anything for a buck." He also said, he "didn't notice any homosexual tendencies in Girvin, but he thought a person of this type could very easily be."

July 30, 1956, Warren voluntarily requested that he be committed to the psychiatric hospital in Nevada, Missouri. He remained there until October 1, 1956. He was classified as "unstable personality." At the time of Ralph's murder, Warren was still on parole from hospital. Parole is the term used in the KBI report.

The hospital's psychiatrist thought Warren's greatest problem was his temper, and although he hated his mother, he depended on her when he got into trouble or needed something. He did not think Warren was apt to have homicidal tendencies and had no opinion as to whether or not he might be homosexual.

Both the Raytown physician and the psychiatrist remarked on the possibility of Warren engaging in homosexual activities. The physician said he had not noticed any homosexual tendencies in him but did not discount the possibility. The psychiatrist did not have an opinion. Their comments appear to have been in response to questions by the KBI agents. There is no indication why the investigators wanted to know if Warren engaged in homosexuality activity. At the time, sexual contact between men was a criminal offense and considered a mental illness.

Investigators probably had questions about Ralph's sexuality—a life-long unmarried man with no romantic connections to women found murdered in a rented car. According to the KBI file, those interviewed by investigators described Ralph as a quiet, conservative, deeply religious man. This description was certainly in keeping with Ralph's background and how his family knew him. None of this, however, precludes the possibility that he had engaged in homosexual activity, perhaps only rarely and unknown to anyone. He certainly would not have been the first man to keep his sexual activities secret. In Kansas during the 1950s, any suggestion of homosexuality could get a man fired from his job, socially ostracized, beaten, or killed.

On May 15, 1956, Agent Lansdowne wrote, "At the time of this report we have more or less cleared Warren Girvin of this crime." He came to this "soft" conclusion despite there being no mention in the KBI file of what Warren was doing during the time he was off work from April 17 to April 22, except for his being at his parents' home in Wichita early April 20.

At the end of the KBI file is a memorandum dated April 17, 1958, from Director Logan Sanford to the Wichita Police Department requesting the fingerprints and the latest photograph of W. A. Girvin. This meant the KBI was still

Warren Arthur Girvin

interested in Warren Girvin almost a year after KBI agents had "more or less cleared" him of Ralph's murder. The same date, Director Sanford sent a copy of Warren's record to the safety director of the Highways Carriers Association in Kansas City, Missouri. There is no further information about Warren.

Ralph Howell Campbell

A burglar with a penchant for women's lingerie, perfume salesman Ralph Howell Campbell was certainly the most colourful of the serious suspects in Ralph's murder. On April 30, 1957, 11 days after the discovery of Ralph's body, Mr. Campbell, age 52, was arrested for burglary in Wichita. At police headquarters, he was found to be wearing a pink silk slip under his regular clothing (see "Appendix 2: Cross-Dressing"). Mr. Campbell had acquired the slip during one of the scores of home burglaries he had committed during his weekly sales trips for a national perfume company in southeastern Kansas and nearby parts of Oklahoma.

The burglaries started in 1952, the same year he arrived in Wichita. When arrested, Mr. Campbell admitted to committing 40 burglaries in Wichita and neighbouring areas. The Wichita police said the total could be as high as 100. The first break for police came four years later in 1956, when an Oklahoma resident spotted a burglary in progress and noted the licence plate of the getaway car.

After more than a year of investigation by Wichita Detectives Cox and Moffitt and KBI and FBI agents, Mr.

Ralph Howell Campbell

Campbell was arrested. A member of the Sedgwick County Auxiliary Fire Department, he was assisting in the search for the body of 19-month-old Earl Berry in the Little Arkansas River when he was apprehended. The child and his mother, Wichita residents, drowned Saturday, April 27, when the boat in which they were passengers was swept over a dam in the city. Investigators traced Mr. Campbell from the scene of the drowning to the Berry home, which he burgled.

Mr. Campbell spoke freely to police of his criminal activities in Kansas and Oklahoma and his previous prison records for burglary. In 1930, at the age of 25, he received a sentence of 15 years for burglary and was incarcerated in the San Quentin State Penitentiary. Discharged in 1938, he later served six years of a ten-year sentence for burglary in Texas. He was released from the Texas State Penitentiary in 1950 and, two years later, arrived in Wichita.

Dubbed the "ghoul burglar," Mr. Campbell specialized in spotting news stories of women who died violent deaths. He would check the obituaries for the date and time of their funeral and break into their home during the service. He consistently stole women's clothing, especially lingerie, jewellery, and hosiery. He also took a wide array of other items, including cameras, watches, electrical appliances, rugs, whisky, typewriters, and guns.

A voluminous quantity of stolen goods was stored at Mr. Campbell's small residence at 2920 East 1st Street in Wichita. The basement was literally crammed with items, so much so that detectives needed to hire a moving van to transport the stolen merchandise to a local warehouse. Mr. Campbell told police that he did not sell any stolen items for fear of being caught. However, during a visit to the warehouse to identify their stolen possessions, burglary victims noticed that many of the dresses were marked with a price and size apparently in preparation for being offered for sale.

On April 30, 1957, around 9:00 p.m., Agents Lansdowne and Kline, along with two other KBI agents, Harold Nye and Wayne Owens, questioned Mr. Campbell. They wanted to speak with him because of the proximity of his residence to Ralph's residence and place of work.

Agent Lansdowne reported:

> We felt that they possibly knew each other and due to the character of Campbell we felt he could have been capable of murder.

Mr. Campbell lived on the grounds of Hillside Methodist Church, where Ralph worked, which is located on the corner of 1st Street and North Chautauqua Avenue. Ralph's apartment in the Girvin residence was diagonally across the intersection and just four lots south. It is quite possible the two men knew each other.

Ralph Howell Campbell

College Hill Methodist Church at intersection of 1st Avenue and North Chautauqua Avenue.

The Girvin house no longer stands. The land is now part of the parking lot for a branch of the Dillons chain of grocery stores.

As Agent Lansdowne wrote in his report, investigators had another reason for interviewing Campbell.

> Another fact or reason for talking to Campbell was that we had traced the gun to a pawn shop in Midland Texas and we knew that Campbell had been in Texas. He could have been good for some burglaries in Texas and this gun could have come out of one of these burglaries.

Long Time Dead

Ralph's killers left the murder weapon at the scene, in all probability, knowing it was stolen and therefore untraceable. It could have belonged to Mr. Campbell; guns were among the many items he stole.

During the interview with investigators, Mr. Campbell said he had checked into the Grand Hotel in Stillwater, Oklahoma, the night of April 19 under his correct name and claimed to have contacted Powell's ready-to-wear shop. Stillwater is approximately 129 miles south of Wichita.

On May 23, 1957, Agent Lansdowne drove to Stillwater, where he spoke with Mr. Ray F. Powell, owner of the shop. When shown a photograph of Mr. Campbell, Mr. Powell could not remember him and said that he doubted if he had ever been contacted by him. I have wondered if Mr. Powell may have denied knowing Mr. Campbell because he sold the latter's stolen clothing and did not want to be implicated in illegal activity. Mr. Campbell was obviously familiar with the store because he mentioned it to the KBI agents.

Agent Lansdowne found that no one named Ralph Campbell had registered at any of the hotels in Stillwater during the month of April 1957. Why Mr. Campbell told investigators that he registered under his own name is a puzzle. He was obviously familiar with police investigations and would have been aware his information would be checked. He could have spent the night of April 19 with a friend or sleeping in his car, which would have been credible and for which there would be no written record. So why did he lie? Investigators knew that Mr. Campbell had been in Stillwater on April 16 because he had burglarized a home there that night.

Ralph Howell Campbell

Agent Lansdowne reported:

> Why Campbell lied to us regarding this matter is unknown at this time. This phase of the investigation is continuing.

Continuation of the investigation of Mr. Campbell was not mentioned in the KBI file past the date of Agent Lansdowne's report of May 15, 1957.

> At the time of this report we still have several things delaying us in this investigation. We still have the gun to completely run out. We still have the whereabouts of Campbell on the date Snair was killed to find.

Mr. Campbell was, in due course, convicted of second-degree burglary and larceny and sentenced to five to ten years for each crime to be served concurrently. On August 27, 1957, he was incarcerated as inmate 13293 in the Kansas State Penitentiary in Lansing. After serving six years, he was paroled on August 16, 1963, and discharged from custody on September 19, 1965.

Mr. Campbell's prison record was obtained from the Kansas Historical Society and provides insight into his personal history and character. He was born January 11, 1906 (1905 is the date on his grave marker), in Elmira, NY, and grew up in "a well-kept, above average house" in Flint Michigan. As described in his prison record, he had an "ordinary childhood." He liked school and got along well with parents. He was an only child. At one stage in his early life, he was "very nervous and unable to apply himself," so the family doctor recommended circumcision. The boy's behaviour is reported to have improved after the surgery. Growing up, Mr. Campbell did odd jobs, had a good work ethic, and always had money.

According to his prison record, he had a variety of jobs as an adult, such as working in sales for a brewery, an office supply business, and various companies. From 1950 to 1957, he was a self-employed manufacture agent, and from 1955 to 1957, a member of the Wichita Fire Department, with the rank of honorary chief. Employment as a perfume salesman *per se* is not listed; however, his prison record shows he was a "self-employed manufacture agent" from 1952 to 1957. This is the period of time Mr. Campbell was in Wichita and, as reported in the press, when he worked as a perfume salesman for a national concern.

Around 1940, he married Claudine Ellen Stual whom he met through friends at his rooming house. They had one child. The marriage "was not successful," and Claudine obtained a divorce when Mr. Campbell went to jail in Texas.

The lack of success for the marriage may well have been related to Mr. Campbell's unusual sexual practices and criminal activities. As stated in his prison record:

> Subject's criminal record is very long and upon examination shows a definite MC [pattern]. He steals women's clothing and hides it. When asked what disposition he

makes of it he spoke freely of his desire and actions. He steals women's clothing for the sex reaction he gets from same. He likes to wear it at night when alone. He states that at this time he enjoys masturbation and practices it by the hour. When asked why he didn't buy clothing with which to practice his unique sex act instead of stealing it, he stated that in order to get his reaction the clothing had to be originally worn by someone he had seen and desired. He likes to take these clothes to bed with him, it makes him feel close to the person he has seen wearing them. [Note: This is contrary to his behaviour as the "ghoul burglar," where he selected a victim's house to burglar after reading her obituary in the paper.] He states that this feeling has been with him since he was a young man and that it still has a strange hold on him. He states that at his age [52] he is beginning to lose his sex desire and that he believes in time he will be able to control his urge to commit theft for women's clothing.

Prison officials, Mr. Campbell's father, and even Mr. Campbell himself thought otherwise. Under the section titled "Prognosis," it is written:

> Subject has little or no chance of rehabilitation. He states that he would probably revert to his old behavior pattern if he were released. His father stated: "I will guarantee unless he has proper treatment, his time with you will be useless."

Agent Lansdowne thought that due to his character, Mr. Campbell would have been capable of murder. However, nothing in his record indicates violent tendencies and in the Impression section of his prison record it is stated:

> Not dangerous and will adjust to penal custody readily.

He apparently adjusted well to prison life and seems to have been a model inmate who performed work at an above-average level, accepted authority and responsibility, and received incentive pay. There is no mention in the prison record of any form of altercation with other inmates or prison staff.

His last known place of residence was in Sebastian, Arkansas. He died in March 1981 and was interned at Restland Memorial Park, Chapel Gardens Mausoleum, Dallas, Texas.

There are many examples of men who indulge in cross-dressing with fetishes for women's underwear eventually committing violent crimes, including murder. Agent Lansdowne would have known of this potential for an increase in severity of crimes.

Ralph Howell Campbell

A notorious case of a cross-dressing serial killer occurred in Wichita, beginning in 1974 with the first victims of Dennis Rader, known as the "BTK killer." The moniker comes from Mr. Rader's own words of "bind them, torture them, kill them, BTK." After a 31-year killing spree in which Mr. Rader taunted police and terrorized the public, he was arrested in 2005 and was charged with ten counts of first-degree murder. He is now serving ten life sentences in the El Dorado Correction Facility, El Dorado, Kansas. Mr. Rader's story is told in the book *Inside the Mind of BTK*, written by legendary FBI profiler John Douglas.[1]

There are interesting similarities between Mr. Rader's behaviour, as accounted by Mr. Douglas, and Mr. Campbell's. On the surface, the BTK killer had an ordinary childhood, as did Mr. Campbell, but what was happening underneath was a different matter. Mr. Rader started having bizarre thoughts at age three, and as he grew, he would hang stray animals. There is no record of Mr. Campbell killing animals. For whatever reason, as a youngster, he was very "nervous and unable to apply himself."

Both Mr. Rader and Mr. Campbell received sexual gratification from dressing in women's lingerie. While wearing frilly undergarments, Mr. Rader would engage in autoerotic asphyxia, a practice whereby self-induced decrease in oxygen, such as strangulation, leads to intensification of sexual pleasure. Mr. Campbell masturbated while wearing lingerie, but there is no mention in the record that he also practised autoerotic asphyxia. Mr. Rader stole some of the outfits he used from the lingerie drawers of his murder victims, and Mr. Campbell obtained intimate women's apparel during his burglaries.

In his BTK book, Mr. Douglas discusses the association between religion and serial killers, such as with Mr. Rader, who was the president and long-time active member of his church congregation all the while murdering unsuspecting people. Mr. Campbell was raised as a Protestant, and as a child, he attended church and Sunday School regularly. In Wichita, he rented accommodations on the grounds of the Hillside Methodist Church. While incarcerated in Kansas, he converted to the Roman Catholic faith in March 1959.

In October 1960, the Catholic Chaplain wrote in a special progress report to the Clemency (parole) Board:

> This man has definitely changed his way of living, has a new outlook on life, and is deserving of an opportunity to return to society.

Parole was denied at that time. Three years later, Mr. Campbell was released.

John Lawrence Faith

John Lawrence Faith was arrested for vagrancy and intoxication on the night of May 12, 1957, in Independence, Kansas. The town, named in commemoration of the Declaration of Independence, is located 114 miles southeast of Wichita and, at the time of Faith's arrest, had a population of about 11,000.

The next day, Agent Kline and Sheriff Floyd Huggins of Montgomery County interrogated Mr. Faith at the sheriff's office concerning his whereabouts on April 18 and 19. Mr. Faith said he had hitchhiked from Dodge City to Garden City on April 18 and described a truck stop in Garden City, where he stayed until approximately midnight. Mr. Faith stated he spent that night with an old bachelor. Garden City is 219 miles west of Wichita and 52 miles from Dodge City.

KBI Agent Alvin Dewey, a resident of Garden City, found that the information Mr. Faith had given about his activities was correct. A waitress at the truck stop café in Garden City identified him, presumably from a photograph, and said he had been in the café from 5:00 p.m. to 11:00 p.m. on April 18.

Long Time Dead

The following day, April 19, at approximately 5:00 pm, he was arrested under the name of John Carr by the Garden City police and was jailed for the night. Garden City police verified the arrest and date.

On receipt of the above information, Agent Kline concluded that Mr. Faith could no longer be considered a suspect.

Although of questionable character, Mr. Faith told the truth to investigators, whereas both Ralph Snair, known as a conservative, religious man, and Ralph Campbell, a convicted cross-dressing burglar, did not always tell the truth. From KBI reports, Snair apparently lied about aspects of his trip to Enid, Oklahoma, on March 29, 1957, and Mr. Campbell about his whereabouts on the night of April 19, 1957.

Why Mr. Faith was considered a suspect is not known, but it does raise intriguing aspects of the case. The fact that the Independence Sheriff's Office contacted the KBI meant the bureau had disseminated information that Mr. Faith was wanted for questioning. This was likely accomplished by means of a widely distributed bulletin. There may have been other names on the bulletin.

Agent Kline does not mention why Mr. Faith was of interest. Warren Girvin was the son of Ralph's landlords and had a long criminal history. Ralph Campbell, a convicted cross-dressing burglar, could have known Ralph because he lived near him and on the grounds of the church where he worked. It is obvious why those two men would be suspects. But why Mr. Faith?

Mr. Faith's Criminal History Record Information, file number 3442, was obtained from the KBI. His arrest in

John Lawrence Faith

Independence for vagrancy and intoxication was the latest in a decades-long series of arrests and convictions. Prior to Ralph's death, Mr. Faith's encounters with the law consisted primarily of drunkenness, grand larceny, and writing worthless checks. After April 19, 1957, he was in prison from June 29, 1965, to April 4, 1969, for obtaining a prescription drug by fraudulent means for resale. This raises the question of whether or not he was involved in the distribution of drugs—prescription or illicit—before Ralph's death. Such activity could possibly have overlapped with the activities of Ralph's killers.

The KBI file contains information on only three suspects. The investigation of Warren Girvin comprises the most extensive report of the three. Ralph Campbell is mentioned only once in any detail; however, due to the widespread and sensational nature of his burglaries, he received considerable coverage in the press. John Faith warranted a report of less than one page and no mention in newspapers.

Agent Lansdowne reported on April 23, 1957, "Many leads were run out and so far it seems to be just the process of elimination." Over a year later, Agent Kline wrote to Ralph's brother Roland, "At the onset of a case a complete investigation is made and all leads are followed, which has been done in this case. We have gone as far as we can without further information." Whatever reports may or may not have been made about the "leads" are not in the existing KBI file.

Sheriff Morford may have interviewed suspects without such information being recorded by the KBI. As mentioned previously, any written accounts that may have existed in the sheriff's office have been lost.

The Mysterious Mr. Weasner

The man known only as Weasner is a mysterious thread woven through the story of the last weeks of Ralph's life. His reappearance in Ralph's life marked a turning point that may have led to his murder. The only information I found about Mr. Weasner came from brief comments made by Ralph, a memory of Ralph's sister, and scant mention in newspapers.

What is known of Ralph's behaviour prior to the revival of his association with Mr. Weasner matches the description given by relatives and associates—a conservative, deeply religious man with few friends who tithed annually and did not smoke or drink. These characteristics would have kept Ralph away from the types of people and places that might have led him into harm's way. In other words, they would have made him "low risk" for being a victim of violence.

After meeting up again with Mr. Weasner, Ralph engaged in unusual activities—he rented a car on at least two occasions, he apparently lied, and he transported goods

The Mysterious Mr. Weasner

of some nature. After responding to Mr. Weasner's request for help in a phone call, Ralph left only a few clues as to his whereabouts and activities until the discovery of his body, three days later. There may not be a direct cause and effect relationship between Mr. Weasner and Ralph's death, but the possibility is certainly worth considering.

About a month before his death, Ralph told Mrs. Girvin he had met an old friend whom he had known while living on North Main Street in Wichita. Later, Edna recalled that her brother had a friend by the name of Weasner, whom he had known when he lived on N. Main Street, his residence for years before moving to the Girvin home. Nothing is mentioned in the KBI file about why this meeting between Ralph and his old friend occurred. Was it by chance? Had Mr. Weasner sought out Ralph? If so, for what reason? Had they kept in touch?

Most likely Mr. Weasner was the man alluded to as "a friend here in town" in Ralph's letter postmarked March 19 to another sister, Grace. The friend wanted Ralph to go to Enid and Emporia. Mrs. Girvin recalled that about the end of March, Ralph told her a friend wanted him to rent a car, go to Enid, and "haul" something back. Ralph said the something was too heavy to bring back on a train or bus, which would have been cheaper than renting a car. Mrs. Girvin and her husband told investigators they thought the friend was Mr. Weasner.

On March 29, Ralph rented a car and drove to Enid. He registered at a hotel using his own name and visited a former employer, Forrest Cameron. On a postcard dated April 6 to Edna, Ralph wrote he had been to Enid and visited Mr. Cameron. According to Mr. Cameron's statement to the KBI, Ralph gave him conflicting information about the car he was driving and the identity of his companion. The *Evening Kansan-Republican* of Newton ran an article on April 22 saying police had a tip that Ralph was accompanied by a yet-to-be identified man on the trip to Enid. On April 23, Agent Lansdowne drove to Enid. He reported, "Many hours were spent in trying to find a close associate of Snair's." Mr. Weasner was possibly the associate Agent Lansdowne had tried to locate.

On April 16, Ralph left a note for Mrs. Girvin saying he had received a phone call from Mr. Weasner wanting him to come to Newton and help him. As previously mentioned, Mrs. Girvin may have known of Mr. Weasner. On April 22, The *Evening Kansan-Republican* reported, "The name [Weasner] is unknown here [Newton], and officers are now of the opinion that the reference was to a Wichita resident. This angle was being checked carefully today." There was no further information in the newspaper or the KBI file about Mr. Weasner.

As requested by Mr. Weasner, Ralph went to Newton, where he visited a private residence in the evening and later spent the night at the Cozy Rooms. On the morning of April 17, he returned to Wichita and rented a car in the afternoon. He made a deposit of $20 and told the attendant he was driving to Emporia on business. Two receipts for gasoline and the odometer reading gave the only information about his possible whereabouts from the time he rented the car until the discovery of his body. Based on the amount of fuel consumed and the approximate miles per gallon, it was possible that Ralph could have driven to Emporia. Sheriff Morford was unable to establish that Ralph had been in the city. If, however, Ralph had not registered at a hotel or other place of accommodation or had not been recognized by café staff, his presence could have easily gone undetected.

Ralph may have been eager to accept Mr. Weasner's request to go to Enid and Emporia. It is known with certainty that the Enid trip involved transport of goods, and it is reasonable to think the same was true for Emporia. Time would have been heavy on Ralph's hands, especially since he had retired, and he would not have had much money. His income was apparently limited to whatever social security he might have accumulated and what he earned from part-time work at the church. The only known significant amount of money he acquired was years before, when he had been discharged from the army at the end of the First World War and when Grace and he sold the property they had jointly inherited from their father in 1941.

The questions of why Ralph rented cars for the trips to Enid and Emporia within three weeks of each other and the source of money to pay for the cars are critical points. No one in the family knew Ralph to rent a car for any reason. Spending the required money would have been contrary to his frugal nature. Ralph undertook the trips because Mr. Weasner had asked him to do so. It seems only logical that Mr. Weasner would have given money to Ralph to cover expenses and to compensate him. It was also stated by Mr. Savniak of the car rental agency that Ralph had considerable cash on him, although it may have been small denominations.

Any thought of possible illegality associated with Mr. Weasner's requests most likely would never have crossed Ralph's mind. At some time, probably after he rented the car on April 17, he may have become aware of the illicit nature of what he was unwittingly transporting. He was then killed to silence him. Perhaps murder had been the plan from the beginning, Ralph being an expendable delivery man.

Drugs were the most likely illicit goods involved (see "Appendix 3: Drugs in Kansas"). There are innumerable ways drugs could have been concealed without Ralph knowing about them. They could have been hidden in items that would not have caused suspicion, such as in the heavy item Ralph was to transport from Enid to Wichita. Or drugs could have been placed in areas of the vehicle, such as spare tire storage areas and dashboards, to avoid detection.

Mr. Weasner may not have pulled the trigger, but there is reason to think he may have been part of a criminal ring, most likely involving drugs, which included the person responsible for Ralph's death. My mother and other family members thought Ralph had become involved in the transport of drugs and this entanglement led to his murder. After reviewing all the information available to me, I think this is a credible explanation.

PART V
Final Thoughts

Two Small Scars

Sixteen words in the autopsy report led me to think of Ralph, not just as my mother's favourite uncle, but as a grown man with all the desires that go with adulthood. Those few words and what they implied led me to explore social attitudes and medical practices of the late 19th and first half of the 20th centuries—that is, the span of Ralph's life. What I uncovered was surprising and sometimes shocking.

In the General Inspection section of his report Dr. Neudorfer wrote:

> There are two small well healed scars in the skin of the scrotum on both sides.

Had Ralph had a vasectomy? What other explanation could there be? Dr. Neudorfer did not mention any scars that could have resulted from surgery to correct any genital abnormality or pathological condition. He reported the external genitalia to be of normal appearance. After reading the report, Dr. Khati Hendry, a physician, concurred that the scars were consistent with vasectomy.

Two Small Scars

This simple procedure, which severs the tubes that transport sperm, is today the birth control method of choice for millions of couples. However, it was not commonly used to prevent pregnancy until after the end of the Second World War in 1945, when Ralph would have been 55 years old.

Ralph never married and, to my knowledge, was never engaged to be married or had a serious girlfriend. There were family stories of various romances of members of Ralph's generation, but not a word about him. It is highly unlikely he engaged in casual encounters. He was raised in a strict religious environment, and premarital and extramarital sex were forbidden. So why did he have a vasectomy? The answer may be related to visits he made to health facilities in the early 1920s.

I knew from postcards that Ralph had sought treatment at the World's Dispensary Medical Association in Buffalo, New York, and the Battle Creek Sanitarium in Battle Creek, Michigan. He did not say in the postcards why he went to either. The leaders of both facilities trained decades before Ralph was a patient and carried with them the attitudes toward sexual activity of an earlier time. Advances in medical treatment had been made at Buffalo and Battle Creek, but some treatment practices, especially those related to sexual function, are now considered ineffective, bizarre, and cruel.

Dr. Vaughn Ray Pierce, founder of the World's Dispensary Medical Association, graduated from the Eclectic Medical College in Cincinnati in 1862. Eclectic medicine was an extension of early American herbal medicine and a direct reaction to barbaric medical practices of the time. The World's Dispensary Medical Association was the name given to Dr. Pierce's medical empire at the time of its incorporation in 1883. The empire started with Dr. Pierce, an entrepreneur of considerable skill, establishing himself as a leading manufacturer and seller of mail-order patent medicines.

To meet the huge demand for his medicines, Dr. Pierce built the World's Dispensary Building at 664 Washington Street in Buffalo. In 1878, he established Pierce's Palace Hotel to accommodate the many patients who sought his skills. The building burned down in 1881 and was quickly replaced by the Invalids' Hotel and Surgical Institute, one of the best-known sanitariums of its kind in the country. Patients came from all over the United States and Canada; in 1921, Ralph was among them.

Dr. John Harvey Kellogg, director of the Battle Creek Sanitarium, studied medicine in the 1870s at three institutions, the last being the well-respected Bellevue Hospital Medical College in New York. In contrast to Dr. Pierce, whose financial interests in his medical endeavours were considerable, Dr. Kellogg was motivated solely by promoting healthy living practices based on the teachings of the Seventh Day Adventist Church. He pursued advancement in all branches of medicine, invented a vase array of medical equipment, and performed thousands of operations without financial compensation. Due to his long-standing interest in the nutritional properties of milk and milk substitutes, he was a pioneer in what we now call probiotics. Ralph mentioned he was on a milk diet in his postcard from Battle Creek postmarked February 1, 1924.

Two Small Scars

Both the Buffalo and Battle Creek facilities stridently warned against masturbation, usually referred to it as self-abuse or the solitary vice, and same sex relationships. The "war" against masturbation began in the 18th century and continued well into the 20th century. Masturbation was considered the root cause of many physical and mental problems through the loss of semen. The practice was also alleged to cause nearly all societal ills from rape, divorce, poverty, and criminal activity to venereal disease, heart disease, nervousness, insanity, idiocy, and even death.

An early crusader against masturbation, the Reverend Sylvester Graham (1794–1851) was a significant contributor to the masturbation scare in antebellum America. He believed that drinking pure water, adhering to a strict vegetarian diet, and consuming bread made from coarsely ground whole flour would help stave off the impure thoughts that led to masturbation. He developed a special process for milling whole-wheat floor, the basis for the now widely consumed crackers.

As popular as Graham crackers have become, the preacher's most significant contribution was through his influence on Dr. Kellogg, who created a cereal he called granola. Following the cereal's success at the Battle Creek Sanitarium, Dr. Kellogg and colleagues formulated flaked cereals. The story of this discovery that revolutionized American breakfasts, the relationship between Dr. Kellogg and his brother, Will, and Dr. Kellogg's leading role in the eugenics movement is told in "Appendix 4: The Tale of Two Brothers and the Taste of Corn Flakes."

Dr. Kellogg, who considered masturbation to be the most debilitating sexual activity, believed it could be identified by 39 signs, including premature and defective development, low mental capacity, mock piety, and eating clay slate pencils and chalk. If bandaging the hands did not prevent a young man from masturbating, Dr. Kellogg would circumcise him without an anaesthetic. For those who continued such practices, Dr. Kellogg performed a barbaric operation where silver sutures or wires passed through the foreskin as it was drawn over the glans penis to prevent erections. For young women, a blistering agent, such as pure carbolic acid, was applied to the clitoris to inhibit any consideration of self-stimulation. When the application of irritating and blistering agents to sensitive parts did not work, Dr. Kellogg recommended surgical removal of the clitoris and labia minor.

In his 1884 book[1], Dr. Pierce summarized the policy of the Invalids' Hotel and Surgical Institute relating to masturbation.

> To those acquainted with our Institutions, it is hardly necessary to say that the Invalids' Hotel and Surgical Institute, with the branch established at No. 3 New Oxford Street. London, England, have, for many years, enjoyed the distinction of being the most largely patronized and widely celebrated Institution in the world for the treatment and cure of those affections which arise from **youthful**

Two Small Scars

> **indiscretions and solitary practices.**
> (Bold font by Pierce).
>
> We many years, ago, established a Special Department for the treatment of these diseases, under the management of some of the most skilled physicians and surgeons of our staff.

Dr. Harry C. Sharp, regarded as the father of vasectomy, was the medical director of the Indiana state reformatory for youthful offenders.[2] He claimed to have performed 175 vasectomies between 1899 and 1907 for the sole purpose of relief from the habit of masturbation. Vasectomy was preferred over the mutilating procedure of castration.

Masturbation and homosexual activity were thought to be interrelated in ways no longer supported. Richard von Krafft-Ebing, a psychiatrist, who first used the term "homosexual" in 1886, wrote that in some cases homosexual desire was the result of the early practice of masturbation and that sometimes homosexuality could be treated through prevention of masturbation.[3] Many early writers, including doctors Pierce and Kellogg, referred to homosexual activity in euphemistic terms. Regardless of the terms employed, homosexuality was considered a medical disorder. The recommended cures, all drastic measures, were castration and vasectomy, LSD, shock therapy, and as late as 1951, lobotomy.[4,5]

Doctor Kellogg and Sharp, along with most of the medical establishment of the day, were also leading proponents of eugenics, which was widely accepted as the means of race improvement in the United States until the Second World War. As early as 1881, Dr. Kellogg attributed what he considered race degeneracy to physically inactive boys and girls who sapped their strength by indulging in "the secret sin and kindred vices." Dr. Sharp championed vasectomy as a quick and easy way to prevent reproduction in undesirables, such as imbeciles, criminals, and perverts, including homosexuals.

In the initial assessment, doctors at the Invalids' Hotel and Surgical Institute and the Battle Creek Sanitarium asked incoming patients about their life and social circumstances, physical symptoms from aches to urination patterns, and sexuality. Psychological and emotional issues were also probed. Whatever led to Ralph's vasectomy, if it was done at either facility, could have been discussed at this time.

As a healthy young male, Ralph would have had to deal with his sexual impulses in some manner. It is unknown if Ralph was concerned about masturbation. But it is known that the army medical corps during the First World War told soldiers to masturbate rather than visit prostitutes, a common source of venereal diseases. While in the army, he certainly would have had opportunities for sex with other men. Considering Ralph's strict religious upbringing, any homosexual thoughts, acted out or not, would have caused him great consternation. Masturbation, especially if practised frequently, would have likely affected him the same way.

The sheriff and KBI agents would almost certainly have considered the possibility of homosexuality being a factor

Two Small Scars

in Ralph's murder; he was an never-married older man with no known intimate attachments to women. Comments by two psychiatrists about a murder suspect (see the chapter "Warren Girvin") being homosexual were probably in response to questions from investigators. Any such suspicion would have probably been kept from the family, especially such a religious, conservative family.

Unresolved

Throughout this project I had assumed that Ralph's killer would have been identified if modern forensic techniques had been available to investigators of the day. But this might not necessarily have happened. A surprising number of murder cases are never solved. In recent years, it is estimated that the perpetrators in at least one-third, perhaps as high as 45 percent or even higher, of murders committed across the United States are never identified. Several factors underlie this unfortunate state of affairs; some are relevant to this case.

Ralph's murder appears to have been premediated. Whether through careful planning or by sheer luck, his killers did several things that helped to ensure they would not be caught. The killing occurred in the very early hours of the day, when most people are asleep, minimizing the chances of anyone coming across the scene. They did not move the body or try to hide it, which would reduce the possibility of inadvertently leaving incriminating evidence.

The killers chose a .22 calibre revolver, a reliably lethal weapon, which would not cause blood to spray and brain matter to splatter as would more powerful firearms. This would prevent contaminating their clothes with evidence. They also wiped the revolver clean of fingerprints and left it at the scene. There would be no telltale fingerprints, and no "smoking gun" would ever be found in their possession. The killers probably knew investigators would hit a dead-end trail when tracing the ownership of the revolver; they would not be associated, even indirectly, with the murder weapon.

It appears the killers may have intentionally left clues to mislead investigators, that is, staged the scene. The revolver found in Ralph's lap may have been placed there to suggest suicide. His pockets were turned inside out, and his billfold was thrown into a nearby ditch with the possible intention of leading investigators to think robbery was the motive. The killers also organized a get away method that left no trace, or at least none recorded in the existing KBI file or mentioned in newspapers.

Today, over half of murder victims are killed by someone they knew. Based on this and assuming the same was true six decades ago, Ralph probably knew one or more of his killers or the person who had sent them. It seems likely that they were part of a criminal ring and were not hired killers. Hiring killers means more people are involved and, thereby, increases the chances of identification, eventually leading to the conviction of the person who hired them.

Understaffed law enforcement agencies are commonly cited as a major cause for murders going unsolved. In the KBI file, only one person, Undersheriff Walter Hillman, is mentioned assisting Sheriff Morford and only that he had attended the scene. On the other hand, six KBI agents and the director are mentioned. Agent James Kline assisted by Agent Paul Lansdowne were the main KBI investigators. Four other agents—Harold Nye, Alvin Dewey, Howard Docker, and Wayne Owens—contributed to the investigation. Logan H. Sanford, the agency director from 1957 to 1969, would have been ultimately in charge of the case.

Agents Dewey, Nye, Docker, and Owens were later involved in the case of the 1959 murder of the Herbert Clutter family on their farm near Holcomb in Western Kansas. Agent Dewey oversaw the investigation of one of Kansas's most famous crimes, while Agent Nye did the bulk of the investigative field work assisted by agents Docker and Owens. The sensational murder, as recounted by Truman Capote,[1] continues to captivate attention and invite scrutiny. Agent Nye's son, Ronald R. Nye, and Gary McAvoy provide evidence that robbery was not the motive for the family's slaughter, rather something more sinister possibly involving both state and federal levels of government.[2]

The KBI was created in 1939 in response to widespread lawlessness occurring throughout the Midwest during the Great Depression. Lou Richter was its first director followed by Logan Sanford and, in 1969, Harold Nye. With only ten agents at its inception, the bureau received requests for assistance from all over Kansas. In 1955, the KBI was handling about one thousand cases per year and hired the largest group of agents since its inception. Among them were agents Dewey, Nye, and Docker.

Under the jurisdiction of the Kansas attorney general's office, the KBI can proceed with investigations only upon direct referral from the attorney general or by invitation

Unresolved

from local law enforcement agencies. The law does not give the KBI more power than a sheriff. County sheriffs are the most powerful law enforcement officials in the state. Sheriff Weldon Morford was in charge of Ralph's case; the KBI agents assisted at his request. This fact may not be apparent in this book because a considerable amount of information was obtained from the KBI and none from the sheriff. The KBI, however, does have broader jurisdictional and investigative capabilities in any area of law enforcement anywhere in the state and across state lines.

The fragmentary nature of the KBI file I examined and the unavailability of the sheriff's file gives rise to intriguing questions. I wonder what Sheriff Morford and the KBI agents knew that is not in the existing files.

Among the unanswered questions are:

- How did the killer(s) leave the scene?
- Where were the car keys when Ralph's body was discovered?
- Did anyone tamper with the scene before investigators arrived?
- What is the explanation for the unusual pattern of live and expended bullets in the gun's cylinder? When, where, and why were the expended bullets fired?
- Where were Warren Girvin and Ralph Campbell at the time of the murder? Both men were serious suspects, yet there is no accounting in the KBI file of their locations on April 18–19, 1957. Mr. Campbell even lied about his whereabouts.

Long Time Dead

- Who was Mr. Weasner and how hard did investigators try to locate him? Why is his first name never mentioned?
- The arrest of John Lawrence Faith leads us to think there may have been more evidence than recorded in the existing KBI file. Why were the KBI agents interested in him and what did they know that was not mentioned in the file?
- How many people did the KBI consider as potential suspects?
- Agent Kline told Ralph's brother Roland that a bullet had been found in Ralph's overnight bag. Why were the bullet and the bag never mentioned in KBI reports at the time of the murder? Did the bag belong to Ralph or to someone else?
- What was the identity of the man who wanted Ralph to sign his brother's name to the note? Did this incident have any relationship to the murder? This question and many others which may seem insignificant should not be discounted because solving a case can start with what appears at first to be trivial information.
- How rigorous were the investigations by the KBI and sheriff? The KBI seems to have carried out a professional investigation using techniques available at the time. But was the same energy put into the investigation of the murder of a 67-year-old bachelor of no particular social, economic, or political consequence as it was into the killing of Herb Clutter, a prosperous socially prominent and politically connected

Unresolved

farmer, and his family? Although from all appearances Sheriff Morford energetically worked the case, his incorrect statements to the press, and the loss of records of an open murder investigation cast doubts on his competence and that of his office.

- Who was the person the unidentified law enforcement agent was referring to when he told Uncle Bob, "We know who did it; we just can't prove it"?

Family Grief

Following a death of any type—natural, accidental, or homicide—the focus is usually on the surviving spouse, children, and parents. Grief following the death of a brother or sister is one of the most neglected types of grief, especially if the death occurs in adulthood. The death of an adult sibling means the loss of someone who was an integral part of your past—common experiences, shared memories—in a sense the death of part of your own history. The death also means the person will not be part of your future as likely anticipated. I was in my teens when Ralph died and did not appreciate, at the time, the emotional and psychological effects his murder had on his brothers and sisters.

The grief of survivors of murder victims is often more difficult to deal with than when a loved one dies of other causes. In the case of murder, death is not only unexpected and bewildering, it is tragic and criminal. In the 2020 book *Wish You Were Here,* John Allore and Patricia Pearson capture on p. 23 what must have been the feelings of Ralph's immediate family.[1]

Family Grief

> Families contending with violent death in a peaceful society have a badly shaken sense of reality. They are constantly dancing in a realm of surreality, even if they don't mention it to others.

The Snair family's badly shaken sense of reality, at first painfully acute, gradually waned over time and the generations.

Some victims' families may be satisfied with the performance of law enforcement and the outcome of the justice system. The perpetrator is identified, apprehended, and sentenced. Although their loved one can never be brought back, they have the sense of justice having been done. Other families of murder victims may experience what they consider to be a lack of justice. They think the verdict is unfair or the sentence inappropriate. The charges may be dropped because of insufficient evidence, or the sentencing may be reduced in a plea bargain. The whole legal process may continue for years with appeals and parole hearings.

In cold cases, families, such as the Snair family, never get the opportunity to see the killer brought to justice. Whoever pressed the revolver to Ralph's head and pulled the trigger never faced a judge and jury for his heinous crime. In all probability, the killer has been dead for many years, taking to the grave the knowledge of the role he played in Ralph's murder.

Despite the police never having apprehended the killer, Ralph's siblings were apparently satisfied with their performance. To my knowledge, they never questioned the competence of the local sheriff and the KBI agents. Ralph's brother Roland wrote in his letter to KBI Agent Kline that he was sure the bureau had done everything possible to resolve the tragedy and his sisters, Edna and Grace, had nothing but praise for what had been done.

Lack of resolution complicates the grieving process. Recovering from grief after murders that have been solved may be complicated by the nature of the crime, the attitudes of society, and the legal system. Grief typically lasts longer than when the death of a loved one dies from natural causes. However, if the murderer is never found, the sense of closure is prevented and the suffering of the survivors may continue as long as they live.

For years, Edna, Grace, Uncle Bob, and my mother would go over the details of Ralph's murder—again, and again, and again—trying to make sense of it. Why did it happen? Did Ralph suffer? And above all, who was responsible? Although burdened with unresolved grief, Ralph's immediate family were reserved and rarely spoke of his death to others.

In the past four years, I have asked myself with increasing frequency why I am writing this book. At first my energies were fuelled by the mystery surrounding an unsolved murder and the adventure of investigation. As the days turned to the hard slog of putting words on paper, I began to question if it was all worthwhile. I am nearing the end of my life, and my sister and cousins are not far behind me. Who else would care? Slowly, I began to realize that I was doing it for *them—the members of my family who loved Ralph.* Like millions of other stories this story forms the fabric of the human experience. Despite the sad memories, it gives me pleasure to have been able to tell it.

Appendices

Appendix 1
Psychological Impact of Military Conflict

The psychological impact of military conflict and the witnessing of death and injury have been known since ancient times. The main character in the *Epic of Gilgamesh*, the earliest surviving work of literature which dates to 2100 BC, was tormented by the trauma of witnessing the death of his closest friend. The Greek physician Hippocrates (460–370 BC), known as the father of medicine, described soldiers who experienced frightening battle dreams. But it was not until the First World War that war-caused psychological trauma was formally recognized by the medical profession and society in general.

British soldiers coined the word *shell shock* for their contemporaries who broke down under the strain of a war fought with new and brutal weapons, primarily advanced artillery, tanks, machine guns, and poison gas. Life in the wretched, wet, rat-infested trenches and the overall siege atmosphere, especially in the first years of the war,

Appendix 1 Psychological Impact of Military Conflict

contributed to thousands of soldiers displaying symptoms such as confusion, nightmares, crying, impaired hearing and sight, trembling, and even paralysis.

In a 1915 paper in the journal *Lancet,* Captain Charles Myers of the Royal Army Medical Corps introduced the term "shell shock" to the medical profession. Myers originally deemed shell shock to be a physical or "commotional" injury related to the severe concussive motion of the brain shaken by explosions. He quickly realized that many men with similar symptoms had not been exposed to exploding shells for months or, in fact, had never been in active combat—in other words, shell shock was emotional rather than commotional.

The psychological rather than physical origin of this life-altering condition had long-term negative implications for many soldiers. They were considered cowards or malingers and denied recognition of their suffering, of any kind of treatment, and of military pensions. Some were destined to spend their lives in jails or asylums or wandering homeless. Among those who were able to resume normal lives, many suffered long-lasting symptoms, among them recurrent nightmares, memory lapses, and throbbing headaches.

Along with male soldiers, female nurses and ambulance drivers also experienced great violence and physical suffering in the war. They were fired upon by the enemy, injured in ambulance crashes, and endured burning eyes from the gas fumes that clung to the victims they were helping. Studies about the impact of the war on women's mental health were unfortunately ignored.

Long Time Dead

Large numbers of soldiers in all combatant armies sustained shell shock. In Britain, the official number of soldiers treated for the condition was around 80,000. In Germany, more than 100,000 men were treated in field hospitals in the first years of the war. Estimates run as high as 300,000 for the total number of German soldiers affected. The number of French soldiers is thought to be of similar magnitude. Thousands of soldiers in all armies did not break down for the first time until years after the war ended.

A few years after the war's end, an estimated 76,000 American veterans had been officially diagnosed with shell shock. In the 1920s and 1930s, the association between deterioration of veterans' mental health, with high rates of suicide, began to be noticed. The American psychiatrist Dr. Thomas Salmon reported in the July 7, 1921, issue of the *New York Times* that 400 veterans had committed suicide in the state of New York alone. Having lost both feet and suffered severe shell shock, Herbert Hayden wrote in an article published anonymously in the December 1921 issue of the *Atlantic Monthly*, that if he had to relive the first couple of years after he was discharged all over again, "he would not face it."

Studies after the First World War and the Iran–Iraq War, 1980–1988[1,2,3] have shown that disorders of the respiratory tract and eyes are frequent long-term effects following exposure to mustard gas. As a long-term complication, development of malignant disease is possibly greater for this gas than for any other chemical warfare agent. Respiratory disorders include persistent coughing, wheezing, and shortness of breath. The physical and psychological scars of

Appendix 1 Psychological Impact of Military Conflict

gassed soldiers could result in a variety of difficulties once they returned to civilian live. It was common for men to be unable to return to their former employment. If they were able to work, they often did so at less demanding jobs. Men who had been gassed often struggled with intimate relationships after returning home.

In 2009, a ten-million-dollar, two-year study by the US Defense Advanced Research Project Agency was made public.[4] The study involved thousands of American soldiers who may have sustained brain injuries from explosive devices in Iraq and Afghanistan. The study's most important findings concerned the differentiation between post-traumatic stress disorder (PTSD), a psychiatric syndrome caused by exposure to traumatic events, and the physical damage of traumatic brain injury (TBI). The results assisted the development of better treatments and shed light on the physical-psychological puzzle of shell shock.

The study reported that brains exposed to low force levels remain structurally intact but are injured by inflammation. This finding was foreshadowed by observations in the First World War that spinal fluid from injured men who had been "blown up" showed changes in protein cells. The protein cells in question are mainly immunoglobins, which have major roles in the inflammation process.

The study also found that patients with TBI may not be aware of their injury because their clinical features, such as difficulty concentrating, sleep disturbances, and altered moods, are shared with PTSD. In other words, someone could have a physical brain injury that looks like a psychological injury.

Appendix 2
Cross-Dressing

The understanding of cross-dressing and gender identification has changed considerably since 1957, when Ralph Campbell was arrested by Wichita police wearing a pink silk slip under his street clothes. This change in societal attitude is evident in many ways. A striking example is the 2019 recruitment ad the British Army ran targeting millennials for undercover roles. In one advertisement, a soldier with bulging biceps and flowing golden locks says as he loads "live" lipsticks into an ammunition belt, "You've got the guts, sunshine; you're really out there, aren't you?"

In 1957, the attitude of the Wichita police and indeed of society in general was in keeping with that of former times when cross-dressing was a crime in many jurisdictions. One of the oldest such laws in North America dates from 1848, when a law in Columbus, Ohio, was enacted that forbade a person from appearing in public "in a dress not belonging to his or her sex." From then until the First World War, 45 US cities created similar laws limiting the type

Appendix 2 Cross-Dressing

of clothing people could wear in public. In effect, police applied cross-dressing laws in ways that enforced normative gender identity.

Cross-dressing laws remained on the books for a surprisingly long time. San Francisco's 1863 law remained in effect until 1974, when ten men were arrested for wearing women's clothing. It took over 110 years to repeal the law in a city recognized as a stronghold for sexual diversity. In less progressive cities, cross-dressing laws are undoubtedly still in existence. Sometimes such laws are veiled as masquerade laws.

In the 21st century, psychoanalysts no longer regard cross-dressing by itself as a psychological problem unless it interferes with a person's life. It is no longer synonymous with being transgender and carries no implication of sexual orientation. In fact, the definition of cross-dressing is sometimes restricted to heterosexual men.

Today, Mr. Campbell's behaviour would likely fall into what psychiatrists call fetishistic transvestism, a term used to describe sexual behaviour or arousal that is triggered by the clothing of the other gender. Some male transvestic fetishists collect women's clothing, for example, nightgowns, lingerie, and stockings, and dress in these feminine garments used for sexual arousal, as Mr. Campbell did. There is nothing in the available records to indicate that Mr. Campbell's behaviour involved dressing in any type of women's clothing other than underwear.

Transvestic fetishism only becomes a problem or "disorder" when an individual suffers anxiety, depression, guilt, or shame as the result of sexual arousal associated with cross-dressing. These feelings may be the result of partner disapproval, which might have been the cause of the breakdown of Mr. Campbell's marriage. The practitioner may also be concerned about negative social or professional ramifications, as exemplified by Mr. Campbell hoarding his stash of stolen women's clothing and other items in secret. To disrobe at police headquarters and the subsequent publicity must have added greatly to the stress associated with his secret cross-dressing.

Appendix 3
Drugs in Kansas

Although Kansas ranks below the average in the percentage of the population using various types of illegal drugs and of related violence, drug trafficking was and continues to be a thriving business. The state's central location in the continental United States combined with its well-developed highway system have resulted in it playing an important role in the distribution of illicit drugs for many decades. In addition to motor vehicles, drug traffickers use the state's extensive railroad system, airplanes, and courier and mail services.

The drugs come primarily from Mexico and the southwestern states, especially California, and are destined for the eastern parts of the country. Interstates 70 and 35 are major arteries in the nation's overland drug trade. I-70 runs east-west in the north-central part of Kansas, while 1-35, the route of most relevance here, extends from the US border with Mexico at Laredo, Texas, to Oklahoma City and eventually to the shores of Lake Superior at Duluth, Minnesota.

Long Time Dead

In Kansas, I-35 connects cities in the southcentral and eastern parts of the state, such as Wichita, Emporia, Topeka, and Kansas City. It is just a little over 500 miles from Kansas City to population-rich Chicago and surrounding areas.

The distribution pattern of illegal drugs is simple in concept yet can be extremely complicated in practice, depending on the drug and the distribution group in question. In general, there are three levels. The lowest level, or retail level, may have a variety of roles—holders, mules, lookouts, muscle. Ralph may have unwittingly been a mule. Wholesale distributors purchase large units of drugs by weight or dollar amounts. Upper-level distributors import drugs in large amounts often from developing countries. They oversee the financing, smuggling, and transport of drugs through transnational networks.

During the 1950s, heroin and marijuana were the most popular illegal drugs in Kansas and other Midwestern states. Today, the most significant concerns in the region are the widespread availability and abuse of cocaine and methamphetamine, associated violence, and the local production of methamphetamine.

Cocaine is smuggled as a powder rather than in the more popular form of crack cocaine because the federal penalties for possession of the former are less severe than those for possession of the latter. Crack is a persistent threat, especially in urban areas, due to its ready availability and consistent connection with urban violence. A derivative of amphetamine, methamphetamine was developed in the 1950s and is highly addictive, often causing paranoia and

Appendix 3 Drugs in Kansas

delusions leading to feelings of fright, confusion, and the commission of violent crimes.

Recently, the prevalence and abuse of heroin has increased due to the demand from oxycodone users, who substitute heroin for prescription drugs, and the increased trafficking of the drug from Mexico. Marijuana continues to be widely available and is of concern because of associated crime.

In Kansas, the number of labs involved in the production of methamphetamine increased until the early 2000s, when high-quality, inexpensive Mexican methamphetamine started to become widely available. Although their numbers may have decreased, local production labs continue to pose safety concerns. The production process involves many easily obtained hazardous chemicals, such as acetone, anhydrous ammonia (fertilizer), red phosphorous, and lithium. These chemicals can endanger law enforcement personnel, emergency response teams, and anyone near the production site, including the operators.

In August 2000, two individuals in Lyons, Kansas, produced methamphetamine and then buried the laboratory under the dirt floor of a farm shed. The laboratory exploded, killing one of the men. The other individual allegedly removed the body and dumped it in a remote cow pasture in an adjacent county.[1]

Wichita has long been a drug distribution hub and a significant consumer market for drugs trafficked by Mexican organizations and other criminal groups. Mexican methamphetamine, powder cocaine, and marijuana are distributed from Wichita to smaller towns, especially in the southern regions of the state and eastern urban centres. This was the situation in the late 1950s and continues to be so today.

In 2020, a 55-count federal indictment was unsealed that alleged inmate Travis Knighten ran an extensive drug ring in Wichita from a prison cell in the Oklahoma State Penitentiary. The ring distributed methamphetamine, heroin, cocaine power, crack cocaine, and marijuana. Mr. Knighten allegedly put together deals with the assistance of another inmate and worked with a treasurer outside the prison and other close associates who collected funds to pay suppliers.

Lower-ranking conspirators were responsible for maintaining stash houses, cutting, packaging, and storing drugs, and reselling the final products. At least five Wichita addresses served as stash houses, including a house on North Chautauqua Avenue, just a block from where Ralph had lived at the time of his murder in 1957.

Appendix 4
The Tale of Two Brothers and the Taste of Corn Flakes

In 1924, while a patient at the Battle Creek Sanitarium, Ralph toured the Kellogg manufacturing plant. The photograph on the front of the postcard he sent to Grace shows several large industrial buildings covering extensive space. Ralph wrote the plant was big and clean, and the food produced was clean.

An international network of healthcare facilities and one of the world's largest manufacturers of cereal foods both originated from the vision of a pioneer of the Seventh Day Adventist Church. Ellen White and her husband, James, were among the small group of members of the new Protestant denomination founded in Battle Creek, Michigan, in 1863. On Christmas Day 1865, Ellen had a vision that the Adventists should establish an institute where members of church and the public could be treated with sensible remedies and be taught how to take care of themselves to prevent illness. Nine months later, the

Western Health Reform Institute was established. Among the first contributors to the proposed institute were John and Ann Kellogg, parents of John Harvey Kellogg and Will Keith Kellogg.

The Whites soon realized that to meet their goals, the Institute needed well-trained doctors and nurses and professional administrators. They recognized in teenager John Harvey Kellogg the potential to provide the needed leadership and partially subsidized his medical education. He joined the staff of the Western Health Reform Institute in 1875, and despite his youth and inexperience, the Whites appointed him medical director a year later. He served in that capacity for 67 years.

Among a series of innovations that the dynamic young doctor launched, the first was renaming the institute the Battle Creek Medical Surgical Sanitarium, commonly and affectionately called "the San." He did not use the traditional term "sanitorium" because he wanted the facility to be "sanitary," a place where people learned how to remain well once they were made well.

The San grew from treating about 300 patients in 1877 to more than 1,600 in 1891. To accommodate this increase, new buildings, including a surgical hospital and an electrical plant, were constructed and a farm was established to supply fresh food. In 1880, John's younger brother, Will, became the bookkeeper and business manager. His business acumen is credited for much of the continued growth of the institution, which in 1885 became the largest of its kind in the world.

Appendix 4 The Tale of Two Brothers and the Taste of Corn Flakes

The success of the San led to the foundation of 27 other Adventist sanitariums in the United States by the turn of the century. Today, Advent Health, a non-profit healthcare system affiliated with the Seventh Day Adventist Church, is part of an international network of 160 facilities, including acute care hospitals, medical and other health-related schools, home care services, and hospices. Hospitals and clinics operate on five continents.

A pillar of the health philosophy at the San was reforming unhealthy eating habits of patients and teaching them about the benefits of a diet of vegetables, fruits, nuts, and grains. An accomplished dietitian, Ella Eaton Kellogg, John's wife, oversaw the development of more than 80 grain and nut food products in her experimental kitchen. When a patient complained she had broken her dentures on the customary breakfast of hard zwieback (twice baked) toast, a search started for a product that was easier for patients to chew and digest. That search led to the launch of the breakfast cereal industry.

Ella, John, and Will experimented innumerable times before learning that the best wheat flakes were produced with thinly rolled, tempered dough baked evenly and with few air bubbles. Will kept detailed records of subsequent trials that improved the process. In May 1895, John applied to the US Patient Office for a patent on "Flaked Cereal and Process of Preparing the Same." The patent covered flakes made of oats, corn, barley, and other grains as well as wheat flakes. Will did not receive co-credit on the patent application, which exacerbated the already difficult relationship with John. A modest introvert, Will laboured unrecognized for many years in the shadow of his grandiose, extrovert older brother. The friction between the brothers over the future of their cereal enterprise increased until it caused an irreconcilable split.

The newly patented wheat flakes were a welcome breakfast treat for patients whose digestion greatly improved. John named the wheat cereal "Granose," and it was sold at the San, as well as by mail order. Soon bakers and workmen were hired, and the production site become a two-story building across the street from the San. The cereal factory operated 24 hours a day. Will commonly worked up to 120 hours a week, overseeing cereal production and tending his responsibilities at the San, its publishing house, and related companies.

For several years, Will revised and improved the recipe for flaked cereals. In his systematic search for better flavour and texture, he turned to corn, which had a sweet, pleasant flavour with the added benefits of being plentiful and inexpensive. Again, endless hours were spent improving the production process. Soon, Will realized that many more people would buy and eat tasty corn flakes for their breakfast than the bland wheat flakes favoured by San patients to aid their digestion. Kellogg Corn Flakes was soon enjoyed by people around the world.

The success of the original wheat cereal did not go unnoticed. Dozens of competitors with products of varying quality set up shop in Battle Creek. Most notably among them was a former San patient, C. W. Post. A failed businessman, 36-year-old Mr. Post went to Battle Creek after enduring three nervous breakdowns and many years of

Appendix 4 The Tale of Two Brothers and the Taste of Corn Flakes

painful indigestion. To help pay his medical bill, he worked in the experimental kitchen, which gave him access to the Kelloggs' guarded recipes. He left the San in 1892 and began to manufacture health foods in Battle Creek. The first of three amazingly popular products, a direct steal from the Kelloggs, was the coffee substitute Postum. He struck gold again in 1898 with Grape Nuts, baked wheat crumbs sweetened with maltose. Several years later, Post Toasties, a modified version of Will's recipe for Corn Flakes, was introduced. A multi-millionaire by the turn of the century, Mr. Post continued to suffer from gastric distress. Despondent, while recovering from an emergency appendectomy, Mr. Post shot himself at his residence in Santa Barbara, California, in 1914.

The sale of Post products and those of other imitators overshadowed that of the San's in the formative years. John, who saw the cereal business only as a function of the health-giving mission of the San, refused to allow Will to expand the business. Understanding the potential of flaked cereals, Will chafed under the restraints imposed by John, the senior partner, who even refused to allow Will office and factory space. In August 1901, Will decided to leave the sanitarium and work exclusively on the cereal business.

In February 1902, a disastrous fire burned the sanitarium to the ground. John vowed to rebuild it and asked Will to raise the funds and direct the rebuilding process. Will agreed to return. John ignored Ellen White's advice to keep the new structure small and simple. An expanded and more elaborate facility was dedicated in May 1903, only fifteen months after the disaster. The continued success of the San's extensive variety of treatments in a luxurious health-spa atmosphere with palatial buildings paralleled the economic boom of the 1920s. Unfortunately, the crash of '29 altered the fortunes of many of the San patrons. With significantly fewer guests in the early 1930s, occupancy dropped drastically, eventually resulting in financial difficulties.

In 1906, Will severed his connection with the San and started the Battle Creek Toasted Corn Flake Company in a nearby modest structure. Under his direction, the business grew into one of the world's largest manufacturers of cereal foods, the Kellogg Company, with over 80 breakfast products.

In the same year, John sold his shares in the cereal business and started the Race Betterment Foundation, a significant driver in the eugenics movement. Eugenics is the concept that the frequency of characteristics considered desirable in the human population can be increased through selective reproduction. In the 20th century, this selection was often attempted by elimination through euthanasia or sterilization of individuals with characteristics deemed to be undesirable.

Among the foundation's activities was the sponsorship of three national conferences that attracted many attendees, including college presidents, scientists, social workers, and business leaders. Three quarters of American universities offered courses in eugenics. In the 1920s, ideas about genetically based racial, ethnic, and gender superiority were considered scientific, modern, and progressive.

The Better Race Foundation along with the Eugenic Record Office in Cold Spring Harbor on Long Island,

Appendix 4 The Tale of Two Brothers and the Taste of Corn Flakes

New York, were funded by extensive corporate fortunes, such as those bearing the well-known families names of Rockefeller, Harriman, Carnegie, and Kellogg. The foundation and record office were instrumental in the United States, becoming paramount in the worldwide eugenics' movement, involving well over two dozen countries. When John died in 1943 at age 91, he left his entire estate to the Race Betterment Foundation.

The American eugenics movement served as an inspiration to Adolf Hitler and other leaders of the Nazi party during the Third Reich (1933–1945) in Germany. Hitler referred to American eugenics in the 1934 edition of book, *Mein Kampf*.[1] He even wrote a fan letter to American eugenic leader Madison Grant, calling his race-based eugenics book, *The Passing of the Great Race*,[2] his bible. As horrific as American forced sterilizations were, they paled in comparison to the euthanasia by the Nazis of millions of people, such as Jews and Roma, homosexuals, and those with physical and mental disabilities. This euthanasia program, staggering in scope, and the terrifying medical experiments of Dr. Josef Mengele were all conducted with the goal of producing the "master race."

Early in the development of his cereal business, Will began to think about how to best use the considerable profits he was accruing. He wanted a charitable endeavour that would reflect well on his family and values. In 1930, the W. R. Kellogg Foundation was established to promote all aspects of the welfare of children and youth, directly or indirectly, without regard to sex, race, creed, or nationality. Four years later, Will fully endowed the foundation with

Long Time Dead

$66 million or approximately $1.2 billion in today's dollars. In the years since, the foundation has donated billions of dollars to worthy causes, advancing the well-being of children and their families around the globe. It remains one of the largest charitable foundations in the world.

Will died in 1951 at age 91.

References

Setting the Scene
1. *In Cold Blood*. 1965. Truman Capote. Vintage International. New York. 343 pp.
2. *And Every Word is True*. 2019. Gary McAvoy. Literati Editions. Bremerton, Washington. 294 pp.
3. *The Forensic Psychology of Criminal Minds*. 2010. Katherine Ramsland. Berkley Boulevard. New York. 303 pp.

Not Just a Victim
1. *Petra*. 2020. Shaena Lambert. Random House Canada. Toronto. 292 pp.

A Pioneer Family
1. The History of Zenda. (No date given) As complied by W. G. Goenner. Zenda Library, Zenda, Kansas.

Changes
1. *History of the Descendants of John Hottel*. 1992. Rev. W. D. Huddle, L. M. Huddle, and Rev. B. P. Huddle. Hottel-Keller Memorial Incorporated. Toms Brook. Virginia. 1183 pp.

2. Camp MacArthur, Waco, Texas. 1918. Loretta Johnston. Amer. J. Nursing 18(8): 697–699.

Dark Days

1. Dust Bowl. 2003. Kansas Historical Society. 2 pp. https://www.kshs.org/kansaspedia/dust-bowl/12040.
2. Kansas in the 1930s. 1970. C. R. Hope, Sr. Kansas Historical Society 36(1): 1–12. https://www.kshs.org/p/kansas-in-the-1930s/13202.
3. *The Grapes of Wrath*. 1939. John Steinbeck. The Viking Press-James Lloyd. New York. 464 pp.

Ralph Howell Campbell

1. *Inside the Mind of BTK*. 2008. John Douglas and Johnny Dodd. Jossey-Bass. San Francisco. 344 pp.

Two Small Scars

1. *Memorandum and account book designed for farmers, mechanics and all people*. 1884. V. R. Pierce. World's Dispensary Medical Association. New York. 48 pp.
2. Vasectomy as a means of preventing procreation in defectives. 1909. H. C. Sharp. J. Amer. Med. Assoc. 53: 1897–1902.
3. *Psychopathia Sexualis*. 1886. R. von Krafft-Ebing. Reprinted by Bloat Books. 1999. ISBN 0965032418. 736 pp.
4. *Gay American History: Lesbians and Gay Men in the U.S.A.* 1992. J. N. Katz. Plume, New York. 770 pp.
5. *Gay/Lesbian Almanac. A New Documentary*. 1983. J. N. Katz. Harper & Row. New York. 764 pp.

Unresolved

References

1. *In Cold Blood*. 1965. Truman Capote. Vintage International. New York. 343 pp.
2. *And Every Word is True*. 2019. Gary McAvoy. Literati Editions. Bremerton, Washington. 294 pp.

Family Grief

1. *Wish You Were Here*. 2020. John Allore and Patricia Pearson. Random House Canada. Toronto. 355 pp.

Appendix 1 Psychological Impact of Military Conflict

1. Long-term effects of chemical weapons. 2002. G. N. Volans and L. Karaillliedde. The Lancet. Vol. 360. Dec. 1. Special issue Gas. DOI: 10.1016/s0140-6736(02)11813-7.
2. The Quality of Life of Mustard Gas Victims: A Systemic Review. 2017. M. Satkin, M. Ghanel, A. Ebadi, S. Allahverdi, and M. Elikaei. Tanaffos 16(2): 116-126. PMCID: PMC5749324.
3. Sexual dysfunctions in chemical injured veterans. 2008. H. Ranjbar Shayan, K. Ahmadi, and F. Raeisi. J. Military Med. 10(2): 99–106.
4. World War I: 100 Years Later. The Shock of War. 2010. Caroline Alexander. Smithsonian Magazine. https://www.smithsonianmag.com/history/the-shock-of-war-55376701/.

Appendix 3 Drugs in Kansas

1. National Drug Intelligence Center. Kansas Drug Threat Assessment. 2003. https://www.justice.gov/archive/ndic/pubs3/3600/index.htm.

Appendix 4 The Tales of Two Brothers and the Taste of Corn Flakes

Long Time Dead

1. *Mein Kampf.* 1934 edition. Adolf Hitler. Zentralverlag Der NSDAP. Munich. 781 pp.
2. *The Passing of the Great Race.* 1916. Madison Grant. Charles Scribner's Sons. New York. 344 pp.

About the Author

Susan McIver

Susan McIver was born in Hutchinson, Kansas and moved with her family to Southern California as a small child. After graduating from the University of California at Riverside, she earned a PhD at Washington State University. She was a professor at the University of Toronto with appointments to the Faculty of Medicine and a department chair at the

University of Guelph. Subsequently, she served as a community coroner in British Columbia. Susan is the author of hundreds of scientific publications and articles for the popular press. She has also written two books on patient safety—*Medical Nightmares: The Human Face of Errors* and with Robin Wyndham of *After the Error: Speaking Out About Patient Safety*, which won a gold medal in health and medicine presented by the Independent Publisher Book Awards.

The unsolved murder of her great uncle Ralph Snair has been a continuing mystery throughout her adult life.

Printed in Canada